I Could Take His Punch

The Amazing True Life Story of F. Joseph McTernan and

His Dramatic Encounter With Jesus Christ

Copyright © 2012 by John P. McTernan

I Could Take His Punch
by John P. McTernan

Printed in the United States of America

ISBN 9781622304257

All rights reserved solely by the author. The author guarantees all contents are original and do not infringe upon the legal rights of any other person or work. No part of this book may be reproduced in any form without the permission of the author. The views expressed in this book are not necessarily those of the publisher.

Unless otherwise indicated, Bible quotations are taken from the King James Version of the Holy Bible.

About the Cover: F. Joseph McTernan at 22. He just arrived in America. The suit was borrowed from his brother Patrick.

www.xulonpress.com

Additional Books

⸺⸺ ∞ ⸺⸺

By John P. McTernan, PhD

As America Has Done To Israel
Israel: The Blessing or the Curse
God's Final Warning to America

Only Jesus of Nazareth Series

Only Jesus of Nazareth Can Be Israel's King Messiah
Only Jesus of Nazareth Can Sit on The Throne of David
Only Jesus of Nazareth Can Be The God of Israel's Righteous
Servant

Booklets

Father Forgive Them (For prison ministry)
My Dogs: Memoirs of John McTernan

John McTernan can be reached by email at
McT911@gmail.com

Or visit his website at:
defendproclaimthefaith.org

His blog at:
Johnmcternan.name

Or write:
John McTernan
PO Box 444
Liverpool, PA 17045

Table of Contents

Preface

Normally, the viewing and your father's funeral are times of great sorrow and grief. This was not the case with my father Francis Joseph McTernan. The amazing miracle that God performed just before he died and my dad's encounter with the love of Jesus Christ took away most of death's sting.

Everyone at the viewing had Joe McTernan stories, many of which I was not aware. My family and friends all knew of my dad's incredible life history and the events that occurred at the end of his life. This was the time when God reached out and touched Dad in a real way.

Knowing I was an author, many requested that I write a book about him and tell his story. This was how the book came to be written. I am really grateful that so many encouraged me to write this book, as I believe many people will be helped to keep praying long term for their own family and friends. Dad's testimony is so powerful that it will help others to make a decision for Jesus Christ to be their Lord and Savior.

I have written many books about Jesus Christ and have travelled across America teaching the gospel of Jesus Christ. I would have loved to have my dad as part of this ministry. Unfortunately, this never happened while he was alive. Because of the miracle God performed in his life, we now have a ministry together, although he is in heaven while I am still on earth. The reason for this ministry is my father's personal testimony which is captured in this book. When I share his testimony, it is our ministry only he is in heaven with the Lord Jesus. What a blessing to share Dad's testimony of how the love of Jesus was poured into him without measure! The spiritual fruit of his testimony follows him to heaven!

Revelation 14:13 And I heard a voice from heaven saying unto me, Write, Blessed are the dead which die in the Lord from henceforth: Yea, saith the Spirit, that they may rest from their labours; and their works do follow them.

I tried to write as accurately as possible, so the events were not exaggerated. His life was so unusual there really was no need to exaggerate anything about him. He really was a unique man in so many ways. He just operated both physically and mentally on a different level than most people. His encounter with God and the manifestation of God's love matched his life. Nothing about my dad was just average, even expressing the love of Jesus in his heart was so unusually powerful.

As I wrote this book, long forgotten memories flooded back to me with great detail. I was laughing and crying sometimes at the same time! It really surprised me how events that happened, when I was so young, were so vivid in my memory. Incidents at a young age can impact us for the rest of our lives. I am very delighted to have such wonderful memories of my father because without these memories this book could not be written.

My mother and father divorced when I was very young. In this book, I write about my mother. Until I am a teenager, when I mention my mother, this is my real mother. When Dad was 55, he married Ann. I became very close with Ann, and in this book I also refer to her as my mother. To avoid confusion, please keep this in mind.

I look forward for the time when the Lord Jesus returns for His church. At this time, the dead will be resurrected first and then the living. Both will be united and remain with the Lord Jesus forever.

1Thessalonians 4:16,17 For the Lord himself shall descend from heaven with a shout, with the voice of the archangel, and with the trump of God: and the dead in Christ shall rise first: Then we which are alive and remain shall be caught up together with them in the clouds, to meet the Lord in the air: and so shall we ever be with the Lord. (18) Wherefore comfort one another with these words.

These verses are very special to me, as they reveal that one day I will meet my father and will spend eternity with him. This truly is a great comfort to me. The hope of the resurrection and being in heaven with the Lord Jesus forever overcame any intense grief for my father's passing. I can say from my heart what the Apostle Paul wrote about death. Through the gospel of the Lord Jesus, the sting of death was defeated!

1Corinthians 15:54 So when this corruptible shall have put on incorruption, and this mortal shall have put on immortality, then shall be brought to pass the saying that is written, Death is swallowed up in victory. (55) O death, where is thy sting? O grave, where is thy victory?

Foreword

This is the story of Joe McTernan. I became a McTernan when I married into the family. I am from West Virginia and everyone I knew were just Americans. West Virginia has strong Irish roots. The Irish settled there, worked the mines, fought Indians, made moonshine, and sang their songs. They left behind their Appalachian music, step dance and folk songs.

I never met a real Irishman, till I met Joe McTernan and his wife Ann. Their brogues were beautiful. I would wonder how an Irish child could ever feel reprimanded with such a soothing melodic language.

Going to New York City to visit Joe opened up a whole new world for me. There were cultural pockets of Jewish, Hispanic, Italian, and Irish people. Many of these people were first generation immigrants who kept their cultures and languages.

I always loved Irish characters in books and movies. They were witty and mischievous, with twinkling, startling blue eyes. They were strong and could fight and box with agility. They could sing, dance, pray and weave incredible stories. Do these characters really exist? After knowing Joe, I can say they truly do!

Are the horse hairs which fall into the Shannon River and turn into eels real? Are the leprechauns dwelling in the misty marshy dips along the Irish roads real? Joe said so! I'd say so too because I would never argue with an Irishman. You won't win!

May this book keep the memory of Joe McTernan alive in his grandchildren, great-grandchildren for generations to come.

Nancy J. McTernan

An Irish Blessing
May the road rise to meet you,
May the wind be always at your back.
May the sun shine warm upon your face,
The rains fall soft upon your fields.
And until we meet again,
May God hold you in the palm of his hand.
Author Unknown

Joe at 12 With His Mother Elizabeth

Chapter One

Out of Ireland: I Was Starving

The incredible saga of Francis Joseph Aloysius McTernan began on March 23, 1917 in Killavoggy, County Leitrum, Ireland. Joe, as everyone called him, was born to Thomas and Elizabeth McTernan. He was the youngest of eight children. Two of his brothers, Thomas and Hugh died early in childhood. Patrick went to America. Two sisters remained in Ireland, and the rest left for America.

His dad was nicknamed Long Tom because he was 6'4" and was extremely powerful. He was the strongest man in the area. There was a contest to see who could move a huge millstone at a restaurant in town. The only one able to move it was Long Tom. This stone became known to everyone as the "McTernan Stone". Long Tom owned farming equipment and a wagon. He had a business hauling materials with his wagon and using the farm equipment for hire.

When Joe was about 10, one of Long Tom's horses was stuck in mud by a riverbank. The horse was hopelessly trapped and dying. Tom had Joe get ropes, which they tied around the horse. Then with Tom's incredible strength, he pulled the horse out of the mud. This extraordinary effort injured Long Tom internally. He was weakened and never recovered. He died two years later. Joe, my dad, was 12 when his father died.

Joe was the only one able to keep the farm going. This was literally for their survival. At 12 he quit school to take care of the family and farm. The farm was in two sections with one located about three miles from his home. This is where the cattle were housed. Every day he ran barefooted to let the cattle out of the barn and then ran home. He ran all year round and in all types of weather. He ran barefoot to save his shoes because there was no money to buy a new pair. In the evening, he again ran to the barn to bring in the cattle. Occasionally at lunchtime, he ran to check on the cattle.

Joe at 15 (Notice the Bare Feet)

Every day for years, Joe ran barefoot for 12 to 18 miles. He was known as the fastest runner in the area and no one could catch him. This long distance running built power and stamina in his legs and developed a strong heart that would carry him for the rest of his life. This became the foundation of his great physical strength.

Handling the farm equipment built great power in his body. At 12, he worked with equipment that was meant for a man to handle. When he was a teenager, he could lift farm equipment and place it on a wagon that would normally require two or three men to lift. Even as a youngster his great strength was evident. Like his dad before him, Joe became the strongest man in the area.

In 2005, I visited Ireland and met with Kevin Harken, Dad's boyhood friend. Even these many years later, Kevin remembered the great strength of Dad. Like so many others, he had stories about Joe and was eager to tell them, especially about Joe's incredible strength.

Joe on Right With His Horse and Wagon

Kevin had watched my father as a young teenager place his arms underneath heavy farm equipment, then lift it up and place it on a wagon. He and others were amazed as it required at least two or three men to lift this heavy equipment, but as a teenager Joe could do it by himself! Joe was very thin without bulging muscles or a powerful looking physique, and no one could explain how he performed such feats of strength. Joe had the power of two men!

In addition to handling a team of horses and farm equipment that required the strength of a man, Joe worked non-stop all day going from one farm to another and moving all that equipment by himself! Kevin just marveled at Joe's strength and stamina. Later, when Dad came to America, many also would marvel at the power of this man, who appeared so thin, and yet so strong.

Dad did not have a great variety of food to eat. His main diet was oatmeal, barley, salmon and cod liver oil. His mother had him go to the fishing town of Silgo and purchase a pint of cod liver oil. He took it every day. Mom would make a huge kettle of barley. He would eat from it all day long. Although, they did not have much, many of the neighbors had even less. Mother McTernan would feed many people in the neighborhood. If the McTernan's had food, they shared it with others.

He lived near the River Bonet which was teeming with salmon. This is where he found the salmon to eat. He became an expert at fishing for salmon, but there was a huge problem. It was illegal to fish for them. The fine was severe along with a jail sentence. Dad had a cousin, who was a game warden, and he would "poach" the salmon when his cousin was working.

One day, he thought his cousin was on duty, but he was off. Dad had a salmon, when the game warden spotted him. The chase was on. Normally, the warden could never have caught him, but Dad was holding the salmon. He did not want to throw the fish away, so he ran holding it, which greatly slowed him down. He ran a great distance, but the warden stayed with him. Finally, he looked back and the warden had keeled over from exhaustion. Dad ran home, and they had salmon that night. He was always careful to bury the salmon bones as the wardens would arrest you even if you were found only with the bones!

Kevin Harken told me about Dad and his fishing ability. Dad was great at fishing and taught Kevin how to fish. He watched Dad also fish with his bare hands. What he would do is stand in the water watching the fish. He would then with incredible quickness reach into the water and grab the fish! We were talking about salmon, which are heavy and powerful! I asked Kevin if my father taught him how to poach? Kevin laughed and laughed and said, "Yes, yes"!

Joe With His House in the Background

I read the book *Paddy's Lament* by Thomas M. Gallagher, which was about the Great Irish famine in the 1840s. (If you are interested in what happened during the famine, this is a great read. At the same time, it is heart breaking to read such intense suffering.) Dad was interested in the book, so I shared some of the information. He learned from his father that the potato crop did not fail for the McTernan family. There was food and the family fed many people and kept them from starvation.

I told him about the landlords who destroyed the homes of those who were unable to pay the rent. The people then built lean-tos from the remains of these homes. They would build them on the property of people who would help them. Dad said that when he was young, the McTernan property was dotted with the remains of these types of lean-tos. The McTernan family allowed many people to build on their farm to survive.

During the Great Famine, the McTernans did everything possible to help the homeless and starving. To read history and then hear from my father how our family was directly a part of these events was stunning. The efforts of the McTernans to help so many people brought tears to my eyes. I was so blessed to know that I came from a heritage that was so kind and selfless.

Dad spoke very fondly of his mother Elizabeth. She was greatly loved by all the neighbors. She was like a mother to many local children and regularly fed many of them. Kevin Harken also spoke very fondly of Elizabeth McTernan and told me how he spent many hours with Dad and his mother in their home. In early 1939, Elizabeth became very ill. Dad's sister Florence wrote regularly to her brother Patrick in America about the illness. A few of these letters survived and one reports the passing of Elizabeth on April 28, 1939. This is a very touching letter, which reports just how much grandmother McTernan was loved. The letter was dated May 2, 1939:

> "Her funeral was one to be remembered. We followed the hearse and the line of people reached a long way and they were as thick as they could walking on the road. All the neighbors paid respect and crowds sat by night at her bedside waiting to the last and the house was not able to hold the people for her wake. It is the talk of the county."

After grandmother died, Dad decided to leave Ireland for America. His brother Patrick paid the passage. He left in October 1939 and traveled by ship on the R.M.S Samaria (II). This was one of the last passenger ships from Europe since World War II was now raging in, and there was a threat of Nazi submarines. The voyage was very tense with fear of a submarine attack.

Dad arrived in America with a very heavy Irish brogue that he never lost. I asked why he left Ireland. He loved Ireland and did not want to leave but said "I was starving". I asked him why he never returned. (He finally returned in 2004.) He said he could not return, and then told an amazing story of when he was in school. The school master's name was Master White. This man was cruel and would beat Dad and the other children. He received many beatings from this man. Dad had vivid memories of the beatings.

When Dad left school, he learned from friends that Master White continued to regularly beat the children. During this time period, Irish schools were known for their cruelty. The day before leaving for America, Dad settled the score with Master White. He gave White a beating that he would never forget, and it would be a long time before White could hurt any other children! Dad was fearful of returning to Ireland in that he might be arrested!

He first came to New York City and stayed with his brother Patrick. (My middle name is Patrick after Dad's brother.) There was little work at this time in New York, so he went to San Francisco to stay with his sister Mary. He found work driving a truck. He hauled thousands of gallons of water into San Francisco every day.

I asked Dad how he learned to drive a truck since he had just come from Ireland. He said there was an advertisement for the job. At the interview, he was asked if he knew how to drive a truck and had a license. He said "Yes," and he was never asked to show the license. He did not have a license and had no idea how to drive a truck. Times were difficult and you did anything to get a job. He was asked if he knew his way around San Francisco, to which he said, "Yes". Although he knew very little about the city, he was hired.

Throughout his life my father was always a quick thinker and a fast learner. He figured out how to operate the truck and then asked many questions about directions in San Francisco. He quickly learned how to drive along with the route through the city. This was his job until the attack on Pearl Harbor when he joined the army.

When Dad went to California, he was shocked to find that he had aunts and cousins there. While in Ireland, no one ever talked about having relatives in California. The first wave of McTernans left Ireland in the late 1890s and settled in California. The only one to remain in Ireland was Dad's father. Then starting in the 1920s, the second wave left which was Dad's brother and sisters. He was the last with the McTernan surname to leave Ireland. The entire family went to America. There are still some McTernans in Ireland, but they are not related. While Dad was in San Francisco, he found that two of his uncles were killed in the 1906 San Francisco earthquake!

Dad was driving the truck, when word came that Pearl Harbor was attacked. People were out in the streets milling around, and he wondered what happened. Immediately, there were rumors that the Japanese fleet was off San Francisco and was going to attack the city. People were in a panic and plans were discussed about evacuating the city if it was attacked. There were rumors daily, and it was difficult to continue at work.

He joined the army and went to Louisiana for basic training on the 155 mm howitzer artillery. The basic training was easy for him, as the running and physical exercise was nothing compared to his life in Ireland. For the first time, he was getting lots of food! He actually liked the army food and was getting three meals a day! He was a natural with a rifle: Dad had fantastic eyesight. In a shooting contest, he won as the division sharp shooter. Dad talked freely about basic training but never about the war in Europe. He never talked about the subsequent injury to his stomach and the ulcers. I tried several times, but he refused to talk.

After the war, Dad settled in the Bronx, New York City. He had various jobs and at each one he learned something new. From this experience, he became a "jack of all trades". He really had great ability with anything to do with building. His main job was building the tunnels under the East River from Manhattan to Long Island. The slang expression for his job was "sand hog".

He worked there for two years and had several harrowing escapes from death. On several occasions, there were cave-ins that he barely escaped. The tunnels were air pressured to hold back the water. Because of the pressure, it was difficult to hear. On one occasion, during the shift change, he happened to look back when he saw a cave-in. The water was rushing towards him without any sound! It was as a dream to him. He warned the others and they just made it into an air-lock before the water reached them. He would have drowned, if he had not looked back! He saw several men die.

He was required to wear a badge all the time saying that if he was found unconscious he was to be taken to a special hospital. This hospital had a chamber for those workers suffering from decompression sickness also known as the "Bends". This happens when, under pressure, dissolved gases bubble in the blood. This is extremely dangerous and can be fatal. The decompression chamber, using 100 percent oxygen, frees the blood of these gases.

Dad was found unconscious three times and after the third time he was fired. It was the best thing that ever happened to him. His friends who stayed working in the tunnels all died in their 40s from blood and bone marrow diseases. Dad was the only one who lived to old age. He believed that long term working under pressure, had a disastrous impact on their bodies and that was why they died so young of these diseases. By being released, he was spared from these diseases.

Although, he was spared, in the long term working under pressure did damage to his lungs. In his 80s, he developed a bad cough with lots of phlegm. He was diagnosed with "diver's lungs". This is a form of emphysema that comes from long term working under intense air pressure. The correct medical term was pulmonary fibrosis.

He was stunned at first because he never was a deep sea diver. Then he remembered working on the tunnels and this was the source of the "diver's lungs". This lung condition would eventually worsen until there was complete lung failure, and the cause of his death.

After leaving the tunnels, Dad worked on high pressure steam boilers. He did this for many years, and it became his trade. He also worked side jobs in the reconstruction of buildings. He did this well into his 70s.

When my father was a young boy in Ireland, his grandfather, Thomas, lived with him. His dad was also Thomas. His grandfather was born in 1846; this was the year the Great Famine began. My father lived to almost 95 and just before he died, he met his great grandson Thomas. This was in December 2011. Thomas is a McTernan family name. In honor of this family name, Dad's great-grandson was named Thomas.

Dad was so happy to meet Thomas. When my father was holding Thomas, a thought flashed into my mind. Dad's life spanned 165 years of McTernans! His grandfather Thomas, who was born in 1846, lived with him. Now he was holding Thomas McTernan in 2011. My father's life touched both Thomas McTernans only they were born 165 years apart!

Chapter Two

Joe and Johnny Mac

W hen I was very young, my mother and father separated and then divorced. I never remembered them together as my mother and father. My earliest recollection of a mother and father were my grandparents, as they raised me until I was about five. My mother left me with her parents and moved to Florida so she could obtain a divorce. The divorce laws in New York were very strict, but in those days Florida was much more liberal. When she came back, I had no idea that she was my mother.

My mother remarried, and when I was about five, she took me away from my grandparents. It is one of the earliest events that I vividly remember. I wanted no part of her and my stepfather. I was born in Bronx, New York, and then moved with my mother to Long Island.

Through all of this Joe was there. Everyone called him Joe, so naturally that was what I called him. I had no idea that he was my father. In fact, I had no idea who my father was. To me, Joe was a good friend who came and went, but was very nice to me. He just appeared and then left only to reappear. There was an amusement park nearby with lots of rides for little children. This is where he spent most of the time with "Johnny Mac" as he called me.

There was great confusion in my life as I lived with my

stepfather, but my grandfather seemed to be always visiting as well, and then there was Joe. My grandparents regularly visited, and on weekends I would often stay with them. I really loved being with grandpa and felt very comfortable with him and grandma. I was much more comfortable with them than with my mother. All of this added up to me really not knowing who my father was, but at my age it did not have an impact on my life.

Joe With Johnny Mac as He Called Me.

Then everything changed in a dramatic way. One day, when I was around six or seven, my stepfather had a conversation with me. At first, I could not comprehend what he was saying. He was talking about adopting me as his son. This was very difficult for me to understand. When what he was saying started to become clear, I asked him if I could still see Joe. He said "no". This did not sit well with me. Then I asked if my name would change, as I knew that he had a different last name than mine. He said "yes". Immediately, everything became clear to me. I understood that Joe was my father and my stepfather was not my father. Somehow, I knew that Joe's last name was McTernan and that was the same as my name. I was John McTernan, and we were McTernans.

My mind was now racing as everything came into focus. I had to make a decision to stay with my father or be adopted by my stepfather. This conversation had such an impact on me that I still vividly remember the incident to this day. It forever caused a dramatic change in my life. I now knew for the first time that Joe was my father. Our names were the same! He was a McTernan while I was his son, John McTernan. Right there I knew that no one or any circumstance would ever change that.

I could actually feel my will come into play. No one was going to change my name from John McTernan, no one. I told my stepfather that my name was John McTernan and that was not going to change. He pressured me about being adopted. The more he pressured me the stronger my will became. I could actually feel determination rising inside me. It was as strong as any six year old's will could be. I was not giving in. Somehow, I knew that if I told Joe that he would stop this and not let me be adopted. I told my stepfather again that my name was John McTernan. I responded to his pressure to adopt me by saying "my name is John McTernan".

I wanted my stepfather to stop, as it was making me fearful. It was real fear and probably the first time I had sensed it. This attempt to adopt me, put a wall up against myself and him, and afterwards, I never felt the same towards him. For a long time, I kept away from him, as I was afraid that he would again pressure me about being adopted.

A special bonding with Dad was forged through this pressure. I had chosen him, and when I did, it meant that nothing was ever going to come between us. I could feel this forming inside me on that fateful day. Something also happened, which caused a dramatic effect on my emotions. It started deep within me: which was the desire to be with my father and not my mother. He was a McTernan: I was a McTernan, and I wanted to be with him.

As I got older, the desire grew stronger. This incident with my stepfather forced me to live against my will with my mother. It hit my spiritual heart extremely hard, and created a broken heart. I can trace my broken heart to this incident. The broken heart caused many problems in my life until it was healed through the resurrection power of Jesus Christ. (I will write about this later.)

As I lived with my mother, she and the rest of the family had a different last name. I was totally isolated as a McTernan. My dad would visit me on Sundays, and he was my only contact with another McTernan. He never mentioned any other relatives. To me, we were the only two McTernans on earth.

When I was about 12, he told me about my cousins. Then he met with my mother and asked if I could spend a weekend with him to visit my cousins. At first, my mother was against this, but I pleaded with her. Finally, she gave in and let me go. I was so excited to be with my dad. This was like a dream come true. He still lived in the Bronx, so just going to New York City was exciting to me. There, I first met my Uncle Tom and Aunt Eleanor and Cousins Mary and Nancy. Their last name was Kelly, but when I found out that Aunt Eleanor was a McTernan, this amazed me!

Dad then took me to meet Uncle Pat and his family. He had five children who were all my cousins. I vividly remember the first time meeting my uncle and his family. He had a wall in the living room and posted on it were all the school awards his children had received. I looked at the names and there was Thomas McTernan along with all his sisters. They were all McTernans! This was so shocking to me. I just stared at the names, and then went to each one and asked if they were a McTernan. I even went to my aunt and uncle and asked if they were McTernans. It was so overwhelming to learn there were other McTernans, and that they were part of my family!

Being with Dad and all the other McTernans gave me sense of real joy and a feeling that I belonged. It created a real sense of peace inside that I did not have with my mother. It gave me a very special feeling that I only had with my dad. In a real sense I was feeling euphoric! This gave me a deeper desire to be with Dad and my McTernan relatives. The downside to all this deepened my broken heart, when I was not with him.

As I grew older, Dad spent more and more time with me on weekends. He knew that I was a big-time New York Yankee baseball fan. He had no interest at all in baseball, but he lived in the Bronx, which was the home of the Yankees. Naturally, he would take me to Yankee Stadium to watch a game. He would pick me up on Friday after work, and if the conditions were right, he would take me to a Friday night or Sunday game. Mickey Mantle was my hero, and I would sit there with my eyes focused on Mickey. How could it possibly be better than being with my dad at Yankee Stadium and watching Mickey Mantle! He would buy me the program for the game. I saved the one from the first game he took me to see. It was on October 1, 1960.

Dad always found something exciting to do. When the Ringling Brothers circus was in town, he would take me. He loved amusement parks, so he took me to all of them that he could find. He would never go on the rides, but he so much enjoyed just watching me. We went to museums and the Christmas show at Rockefeller Plaza. He loved the beach, and we spent many a beautiful day at the ocean.

Dad said that he knew Jack Dempsey, the former heavy-weight champion of the world, and wanted me to meet him.

Yankee Program from October 1, 1960

Dempsey owned a restaurant near Madison Square Garden. After watching an event at the Garden, Dad took me to meet Dempsey. Sure enough, we went to Dempsey's restaurant, and he was there. Dad went right to him and introduced me to Jack Dempsey! I could really tell that Dad was proud of me. Dempsey looked very old but was still powerful looking. He shook my hand with the most enormous hand that I had ever felt. His hands were so big that I was stunned. He was very gentle and said nice things to me. Dad and Dempsey talked for a while.

Dad also said that he was good friends with Rocky Marciano, who also was a former heavyweight champion of the world. At the time, he did not tell me how he became friends with Marciano, but it turns out that he worked for a wealthy man, who was very close with Rocky. When Marciano flew into New York City, Dad's boss would have him meet Marciano and chauffeur him around. This was how he became friends with Marciano. Dad really liked "the Champ" as he called him.

One day when I was about 14, I was at work with Dad. His boss needed a ride home as his vehicle had broken down. He lived in a very exclusive area of Long Island right on the ocean. He also owned a small home nearby, and Marciano would often stay there. Dad offered to give his boss a ride, as it was on the way to my mother's home.

We dropped the man at this home and turned the corner. Dad started to yell, "There's the champ". Rocky was getting out of his vehicle and walking into a house. Dad told me to roll down the window and then yelled, "Champ, champ, champ". Rocky stopped and came to the vehicle right at my window. He bent down, and I was now face to face with Rocky Marciano! Dad spoke with him and then said "This is my son Johnny". Rocky held out his hand: we shook hands, and he said, "Nice to meet you kid". Rocky then started to walk away: Dad was yelling to him "good luck champ". I sat dumbfounded, as I watched Rocky walk away and into the house.

This was just like my dad to be friends with both Jack Dempsey and Rocky Marciano. He was also very good friends with Mike McTigue, who in the 1920s was the light heavyweight champion of the world. I never met Mike, but Dad told many stories about him. A young boy never forgets events like these. It was so amazing to me that my dad knew these champions. In my eyes, this made my dad very special.

In addition to these former boxing champions of the world, I met other famous people through my father. Dad worked at the Academy of Music on 14th Street in Manhattan. This was a large deluxe movie theater that sat 4000. It had the biggest chandelier that I had ever seen and all sorts of ornate fixtures throughout it. I loved to just walk around and look at all the beautiful craftsmanship. Being in this building was just like being in a time warp. Dad operated the high pressure steam heating system. When I would stay with him on weekends, he would take me to his work. I was around 14 at this time.

In 1962, a weekend rock concert was held at the theater. Dad worked on the maintenance for this production. He took me and his dog Teeny with him. To me, this was like a fantasy-land. I was not really interested in rock music, but interacting with all the stars was so strange. Some of the entertainers were Johnny Mathis, Dion, Bobby Lewis, The Isley Brothers, Gary (US) Bonds, The Belmonts, The Chantels, Joey Dee and the Starlighters, Bobby Vee and others. I remember especially liking Joey Dee and Bobby Vee. Both of them stand out in my mind but, especially Bobby Vee.

After a show was over, I was sitting at the drums banging away. I had no idea what I was doing but just making noise. All of sudden standing next to me was Little Willie of Joey Dee and the Starlighters. These were his drums, and it sure looked like I was in trouble. But, he was real nice and said that I had talent! He spent a little time showing me how to play.

**Program With
Joey Dee and Starlighters' Autographs**

I was not really interested, but was just relieved that I was not in trouble. During my lifetime, I never again beat on the drums.

When I told my friends about the weekend, they found it hard to believe and thought I was making it all up. I remember bragging to them about my dad! He had obtained a souvenir program of the show and took me around to get the entertainers' autographs. The program is what I used to prove that this really happened. I still have this program from so many years ago.

Dad loved dogs. His first dog was named Teeny: She looked part Beagle. He found her running alongside a major highway. He stopped the car, and she jumped in. Dad was afraid the dog was going to be killed running so close to the highway. She had no identification, so he kept her. He took Teeny everywhere with him including work!

I really loved dogs and still do. (I wrote the life memoirs about my dogs titled: *My Dogs, A lifetime of wonderful memories.* You can find this on my website.) When I was about 12, Dad called and said he found a pup for me. Some youngsters had the pup and could not keep her. She lived in a coal bin. He paid $5.00 for the pup and had to wash her a few times to find what color she was as the dog was so filthy!

At first, my mother was not interested in getting a pup. My mom and dad did not talk, so I was the go-between over the dog. After a lot of pressure, Mom had a change of heart. My mom also had a soft heart for dogs.

Dad was on the way with the pup. He mentioned there was something special about this pup. I can still remember him saying a few times, "she is a beauty". I was so excited waiting for him to arrive. I can still remember sitting by the front window looking and waiting. Finally, his car pulled up, and he arrived with the pup. She was black and mostly a fox terrier. My dad let me choose the name; I chose Princess. Mom liked the pup and even interacted with Dad.

When Dad came to visit, we would take the two dogs with us. We found places to hike and everyone had a great time, especially the dogs. For the rest of our lives, both of us always had a least one dog, and usually more than one. Dogs and McTernans seem to be inseparable.

When I was about 13, I moved in with my grandparents. This made me very happy as my dad and mother did not have to meet. There was always great tension when they met. I was always afraid that a fight would erupt as my mother deeply disliked Dad. He was always nice and polite to her, but she could be cutting to him. As a youngster, I was very sensitive to this tension between my mother and father. My mother would change noticeably in Dad's presence; to the degree that it frightened me. I was afraid of a fight. After I moved in with my grandparents, they met only once and that was at my high school graduation. This was fine with me.

Now that tension was all gone since Dad would meet with grandpa and grandma. They all got along fine, and grandma came to really love my father. My grandparents were from Ireland, and they would talk with Dad about the "old country". Dad would bring special bread from a famous bakery in New York along with a delicious butter, which we all loved to eat. Grandma would make him special Irish potato pancakes, which Dad loved to eat, so it was a fair trade! It brought joy to me that my grandparents and my father were friends.

My parents never talked to me about the divorce. I knew my mother had divorced my father, but neither one talked about it. I never asked questions because deep down inside I knew that ugly things would be said that I did not want to hear. So, to the day of both my mom and Dad's passing, I never asked them what happened. One day, grandma started to talk about the divorce. She was saying nice things about my dad, and how much she had come to love him. She said that no one had any idea just how sick my dad really was before the divorce. They thought he was lazy, but she came to realize this was not true.

Right after I was born, Dad developed serious stomach problems and often stayed in bed. This continued until 1954, when he was operated on and had part of his stomach removed. The family thought he just was lazy and forced my mother to work. Apparently, this was one of the causes for the divorce. Grandma now realized that the apparent laziness was not true and felt sad for him. This brought joy to my heart that grandma, grandpa and Dad were all friends. There was no tension between them, and I was really happy when they were all together.

As I grew older, Dad and I stayed close. He was a big-time hunter and took me with him. I did not like deer hunting but went just to be with him. After shooting my first and only deer, that was enough for me, as I did not have the heart to hunt. When I was racing cars, he came to watch. Also, there was a bunch of us who lifted weights, and Dad would come and watch. One of my best friends became good friends with my dad! As I grew up we stayed close. I went away to college, but always called him, and when I came home would always visit him.

In the late 1960s, Dad had a serious back operation. He was in the hospital for a long time, and for at least three years afterwards he suffered tremendous pain. He began to drink heavily, which I now realize was a way of self-medicating the pain. At the time, I was unaware of this. His drinking was putting a huge strain on our relationship.

I brought my girlfriend, Nancy, later to become my wife, to meet him. I called ahead and requested that he not drink. When we arrived, he was drunk, and I was so embarrassed that it was painful. Nancy did not seem to care, but rather liked him. He was very likeable. This event started to break the bond between us. I told him the drinking must stop, but he continued the heavy drinking. I was calling and meeting with him less and less. For the first time, the special bond was in danger.

Finally, around 1974, he called and said that he had stopped drinking and was going to Alcoholics Anonymous. This was exciting to me, and true to his word, he stopped drinking. He never took another drink of alcohol for the rest of his life! He also stopped smoking and never again smoked. I was happy, as the unity between us was restored. One day years later, Dad said he stopped drinking because of me. We did not go into details, but I knew he was talking about the special bond between us. He knew the alcohol was driving me away and created a choice between the alcohol or me. He chose me!

In the mid-1980s, I transferred to Nashville, TN. Shortly after moving, Dad had a heart attack. He was 70 at the time, and the attack seemed serious, which it would have been for anyone but him! That special bonding was pressuring me to move closer to him. The Harrisburg, PA office opened, which was just a five hour drive to Dad's place in New York's Catskill Mountains, so I transferred. This allowed me to see him more often and also to take his grandchildren to be with him. It turned out to be a very good move.

When I visited him, he always wanted to take the grand-children to amusement parks and other sites. Just like he did with me, so that is exactly what he did with his grandchildren. They had great fun with grandpa.

Thomas was the frequent first name for my family going back into the 1700s. Dad's father, grandfather and great-grandfather were all named Thomas. He had a brother Thomas who died very young. My son Jesse decided to name his son, Thomas, after the family history. Thomas was born in 2010, but Dad had never seen him. In December 2011, Jesse took Thomas to meet his great-grandfather. Dad was so happy. You could see him light up when holding Thomas. He referred to Thomas as a "lovely child lovely". In my entire life, I never had heard my dad sing, but he was holding Thomas and singing an Irish song to him! This was about six weeks

Four Generations Jesse grandson standing; John son sitting; Liam step great grandson; Thomas great grandson; dad the Patriarch, as I called him

before he died. Jesse took pictures, and I showed them to Dad just two days before he passed. He was absolutely delighted with the pictures of Thomas.

Dad's family expanded to four grandchildren and five great-grandchildren. The decision I made, so many years ago, that he was my dad and nothing would ever separate us, lasted to the very end. We were McTernans and nothing ever did come between us.

Chapter Three

I Could Take His Punch

When Dad was younger and if you looked at his physical makeup, it was easy to come to the conclusion that he was tall and very thin. He was tall, at six-foot, but not thin, although he certainly looked it. His build was very deceiving as he weighed around 185 pounds, but with amazing strength. He did not have a powerful looking physique with bulging muscles, yet he was frighteningly strong.

I first became aware of my dad's power when I met his friends and coworkers. People seemed to be eager and were compelled to tell me about Dad. I would often hear, "Kid, your dad is the strongest person I ever met." I would look at Dad and how thin he appeared and often wonder what they were talking about. They would also say he was as quick as a cat, and no one could catch him in a race.

When I was a teenager, I found out just how strong he was. One day we started to wrestle. I was a big kid, very athletic and lifted weights. At this time Dad was around 48, but his power was like that of a bear. It was shocking to come up against such power. His hands felt like vice grips, while the power in his legs was inhuman. He would laugh as I tried to bend his arm or knock him off his feet. He would stop me with his hands, and I simply could not budge him an inch.

His favorite way of taking care of me was getting me down to the ground and then wrapping his legs around my chest and locking his feet together. It is called a scissor hold. With his great power, the wrestling was immediately over. I knew he had the power to crush my ribcage that is just how powerful he was. The "fight" was over when I hollered "mama".

Actually, there were two ways he ended the wrestling match. The second was for Dad to rub his face on me. He had the worst facial stubble that you could ever imagine. It was like barbed wire. Wherever he rubbed his face, my skin would turn red and burn! It actually felt like fire, and it would hurt for a long time afterwards!

Dad's facial hair was part of his legacy. He always looked like he needed a shave. He could shave three times a day! The mere thought of Dad rubbing his stubble on me made me yell "mama" and beg for mercy. What a choice I had of being crushed in a scissor hold with those powerful legs or burned by his facial stubble. I would take a chance to wrestle and avoid the scissor hold, but would immediately beg for mercy, when he even hinted at using that stubble as a weapon! He only "burned" me twice but that was enough. I was always ready to yell "mama".

One day when we were wrestling, I grabbed his big toe and tried to bend it. To my amazement, it was impossible to bend or even move the toe. It actually felt like a steel bar! Dad just lay there laughing while I did everything I could to bend the toe. I used two hands, twisting and pulling, but it was all a waste of time. He did nothing but just tightened the toe and then laughed at me trying to bend it.

Dad then told me a funny story about his big toe. He had a friend Jimmy Waters and they often would wrestle. Jimmy was a legendary tough guy, and he was no one with whom to tangle. Jimmy had Dad in a headlock, and he could not break free. Waters took Dad down to his knees and was really hurting him, so he faked as if he fainted. Waters then let him loose, and immediately, Dad knocked Waters down and got him in the scissors hold. Dad said he gave Waters the "works", all that he had, and in a desperate attempt to escape, Waters grabbed Dad's big toe trying to break it. Waters had the same result as I did. Dad said the last thing Waters did before fainting was curse the big toe!

I attribute the awesome power in Dad's legs to all the barefoot, long distance running he did in Ireland. For years, every day he ran 12 to 18 miles, and I think the running barefoot developed such power in his toes. The farm work along with picking up the heavy equipment developed his upper body. The combination of his running and the heavy equipment made his body like a steel bar with NO fat on it. Even in his old age, Dad's stomach muscles rippled. It is still hard to imagine just how powerful he was without those bulging biceps!

Along with this great strength of Dad's was that he had no fear of anyone. His friends would also tell me that my dad was fearless. He generated an aura of being fearless. I knew he was fearless, but everyone around him knew this also. The combination of his great strength and fearlessness made him an awesome opponent for anyone who tried to harm him. Dad was not aggressive but simply would not back down. Dad's strength and fearlessness were severely put to the test on several occasions.

I found out about one of these tests when Dad came to visit at grandma's home. Somehow during the visit, I said that Mom's cousin was visiting and mentioned his name, Frank. I had no idea that Dad knew him. Dad exploded in anger as he wanted to go and fight Frank. I was shocked, as I had never seen my father like this before. He was actually cursing which shocked me even more. Dad was yelling and saying because of him I spent two months in the "Tombs" and lost my job. The "Tombs" was a notorious prison in New York City. He said the lawyer cost him thousands of dollars. Many times he said, "I should have finished him off when I had the chance". I had no idea what had happened, but Dad was so worked up that I was scared. I was pleading with him not to go to my mother's house where Frank was but to go home. When he started to leave, I stopped him because I was afraid he was going to make a beeline to Mom's. After the longest time, he calmed down and agreed to go home. I watched him drive away. If he made a left turn it was towards home while right was to mom's. He made a left, and I immediately ran to grandma to find out what happened between Dad and Frank.

Grandma told me this amazing story. When Mom was in the process of divorcing Dad, she had two cousins serve the court papers. One was Frank and a teenager named Jimmy. Frank was a professional fighter, who at one point had a record of 17-0. He fought as a light-heavyweight. Grandpa had watched him fight in Madison Square Garden. In addition to being a professional fighter, Frank was a great athlete. He was the high jump champion of Ireland.

These two went to Dad's apartment to serve the divorce papers. Dad was standing in the doorway reading the papers when Frank said he had something else. He then hit Dad with a tremendous punch, driving Dad into his apartment. Frank followed him in. The fight was on. Frank must have been stunned when his punch failed to knock Dad out or even down! What a fight this must have been, with Dad's tremendous power, and cat-like quickness plus an indomitable will, matched against a skilled, highly trained professional fighter. It was a battle of the ages! Dad was about 35 while Frank was 25.

Dad lived in what was called a five-flight walkup. There was no elevator service but a big open stairway. Dad took the punch and then drove Frank out of the apartment. I am sure, when Frank felt Dad's punching power, he immediately knew he made a huge mistake! The fight was vicious, and they fought down the stairway to the next floor. The fight continued all the way to the ground floor. In the end, the professional fighter was left bleeding, battered, unconscious and with multiple broken bones. A neighbor that knew karate intervened and hit Dad to stop him.

Grandma told me all about Frank's broken bones and injuries. I forget the details, but I do remember it was extensive. He was hospitalized because of the severe beating. Frank did not tell the truth to the police, and Dad was arrested and taken to the "Tombs" where he was held for two months because he could not make bail. The truth was that Frank, an officer of the court, had started the fight. The family was in a real quandary, because Frank was beaten so badly, they wanted my father to go to jail, but because he was my dad, they did not want him in jail. Finally, just before trial, Jimmy, who was with Frank told the truth. The District Attorney then dismissed the charges.

Decades later I talked with Dad about the fight. He did not freely talk, as I think it brought back terrible memories. He did tell me it was horrible in the "Tombs". The bail was set very high because Frank was viewed as an officer of the court. Because he gave Frank such a beating, the DA wanted him to go jail for six to eight years!

I knew Frank was a professional fighter, so I asked, "How were you able to beat him?" Dad looked at me right in the eyes and said, "I could take his punch, but he couldn't take mine". This statement epitomized my father. Few "normal" humans could stand up to and beat unconscious a professionally trained fighter as my dad did. He was just not normal in anything!

Another time, two muggers made a huge mistake of underestimating the thin elderly man they planned to attack. Dad was about 50 at the time, and he was coming home from work one night. It was about midnight and his dog Teeny was with him. The dog was ahead and suddenly stopped. The way the dog acted Dad knew something was wrong. Behind a car were two muggers waiting in ambush. They came after Dad and each had a knife. Knowing my father, he would never back down from the muggers. Dad said the dog saved his life, as she alerted him to the danger and then fought off one of the attackers. The dog was stabbed during the battle but lived.

Joe at 46 with Teeny (Around the Time of Battle)

With Dad's vice-like grip in his hands, he was able to take the knife off the attacker and as he reported to me, "When I was finished with him, he wasn't moving". I can only imagine what happened, when even at 50, Dad possessed tremendous bone-crushing punching power. At 50, he was more like someone who was 25. What terror that mugger must have felt, when he realized the power of my father. The second mugger was bitten by the dog, and apparently, wanted no part of Dad. He ran off.

About a week or two later, Dad was again returning from work and was about to enter his apartment. Once again, Teeny alerted him to danger. This time it was behind the front door. Dad opened the door and then with all his strength, forced the door against the back wall. Dad said the second mugger, who ran away from the previous attack, was now trapped behind the door. Dad put his shoulder to the door to keep the mugger pinned and then began smashing him with his right hand. Teeny got in on the fight and was tearing at the mugger's leg!

When Dad was sure the attacker was unconscious, he stopped punching and opened the door. The mugger fell to the ground, and out of his hand fell a huge knife. The mugger was lying in wait to kill Dad, but instead met the incredible power of Joe McTernan! Dad then dragged the unconscious mugger down to the first floor and left him. Someone called the police, and an ambulance came and took the mugger to the hospital. I asked Dad if he reported the attack to the police. He said the beating he inflicted was enough! With his power it must have been an awful beating. He never heard anything about this incident.

Dad called his nephew and asked him to come with a U-Haul, as he had to move away immediately. He then called me and reported what just had happened. He said, "They know where I live and next they'll kill me". Both of these muggers had no idea who they had chosen as their victim when they attacked my father. From the severe beatings they received, I am positive they never forgot him!

The last story about my dad's amazing power occurred when he was 75. I came to visit, and my mother said, "Did you hear about your father getting arrested?" Dad was sitting across from me with his head down and would say nothing, so my mother told me what happened.

Dad went into a store while my mother stayed in the vehicle. Time went by and two state police cars pulled up, and the troopers went into the store. She waited a while and fol-lowed them in. There was Dad sitting on a chair in handcuffs with the troopers holding his driver's license and laughing.

There was a young man across the room sitting on a chair, and they go over to him. The troopers show him Dad's license. He then shakes his head sideward making a "no" motion. While the troopers are still laughing, they take the cuffs off Dad and let him go. The young man was just 25, and he could not face going to court and admitting that a 75 year old beat him up! He was too ashamed!

What had happened was the young man was smoking. The smoke was getting into Dad's face, so Dad asked him to stop. The man sucked in a deep lung full and blew all the smoke into Dad's face. This was the wrong thing to do. Dad hit him and down he went.

I asked him if this was true. Dad said he did not mean to hit the man, but it was like a reflex. Dad just instinctively hit with his right hand, and as Dad said, "He fell unconscious like a sack of potatoes at my feet". I told Dad he was 75 now and too old for this, and it was time to "hang up the gloves". Knowing the power of my dad, I think that few 25 year olds could take his punch! This was the last event of Dad's "boxing" career.

I once asked Dad if he ever thought about becoming a professional fighter. He had offers to train and fight, but said that he did not like fighting and rejected the offers. This was my dad. He did not like to fight, but he sure was not going to back down from anyone. He really did not have any fear. He was very friendly and it was very easy to become good friends with him. After having met him for an hour, people felt like they were best friends. If you were his friend, he would do anything for you.

As I said before, when I was with Dad's friends they felt compelled to tell stories about him. Dad liked to hunt and I often went with him. He took me upstate New York, including the Catskills and Adirondack Mountains. I would hear stories about what a great hunter he was, and how he would go deep into the mountains where others would not go. The reason he could do this was his sense of direction. Dad could always sense north. He did this without a compass! He knew north by studying nature. He tried explaining north to me by the way the trees were bent by the prevailing winds and the location of growing moss. He also knew north by the location of the sun at noon.

He tried his best to teach me, but I could not see the woods like he did. There was no way I was going on my own in the Adirondack Mountains. He could do it and always seemed to get a big buck. Thinking back on Dad and the way he navigated through the mountains, I really do think he would have fit in perfectly with Daniel Boone and the frontier men.

I spoke with several eyewitnesses who stated they watched Dad walk slowly up to a wild deer. He walked very slowly but steadily. He looked at the deer, who was staring at him. Dad stopped close to the deer and then put out his hand and touched it. The deer never moved, as he touched it. I pressed the people about this, and they assured me that it had happened.

All this created a very strange dichotomy about my father. He lived and worked in New York City, yet he was so natural and comfortable in the mountains. He loved the mountains, and you could see on his face how happy he was in the country. He spent all his spare time in the mountains and eventually bought a small home at the base of the Catskill Mountains. He retired to this home. Many close friends knew how much he loved the Catskills and referred to them as "Joe's Mountains".

Dad was a great shot with a rifle. I heard all kinds of stories about his shooting ability. He had great vision, and it was either 20/10 or 20/15. Even in his 90s, he still had great distance vision. Dad had made a fantastic trick shot and some doubted he could do it again. This time I was with him. He put a dime on a telephone pole and went a great distance away. Last time, he had put the bullet right in the dime. This time the light was poor and he could not see the dime. He told me put my finger where the dime was and then get away. I did as he asked. He yelled, "I got it," and I ran. The shot went off, and I ran to the dime. Sure enough there was the bullet hole in the dime. His friends were amazed, as was I.

For many years, Dad also worked on plumbing and building reconstruction. His friends at work told me the same type stories that so many others had shared. They said that he was the very best at work. Some of the plumbing jobs were very difficult and complicated. Dad could see right away what to do and explained this to others, who could not grasp his vision of the work. Eventually, they learned he was right and knew what he was doing. They then just followed what he said!

Dad's old friend and working partner Tony Kerins told me many stories about Dad and working with him; one story stands out. They were working on a huge three-story brick house. As they started the reconstructive work, it became apparent that the foundation was damaged and extensive repairs were needed. The only way to accomplish this was to lift the house above the foundation. He had never done this before, plus the house was so big. Dad immediately knew what to do and where to place the jacks.

Tony wanted to get an engineer to look at it but he trusted Dad. They placed the jacks exactly where Dad told him and lifted the house off its foundation. If the house shifted and fell, they would have been in serious trouble. Tony said he did it because he completely trusted in Dad, as he understood construction like no one he had ever known.

I was with Dad when he was doing plaster work in an old but exclusive restaurant in Manhattan. Part of the ceiling had fallen from water damage, and it contained beautiful artistic designs. Dad was replastering the ceiling along with recon-structing the artistic designs. The manager was watching everything Dad was doing. Dad would get off the ladder and just like an artist look at his work. This went on late into the night. Finally, he was finished. The manager looked over the work and praised Dad. He said it was fantastic work. I remember the manager saying he knew of no one else who could do plaster work like my father. I asked Dad how he was able to do such detailed plaster work. He said "You had to have the eye for it"!

Dad was an expert horseman. He had learned this as a youngster in Ireland. He lived in the Bronx, NY, so I never watched him a ride a horse. When I got older, he would take me horseback riding with him. He looked just like a cowboy on a horse. One day, we were at a place that boarded horses. Apparently, there was a horse that was giving someone trouble and the man was hitting the horse. Dad was very upset and went to the man. Next thing I know, Dad was on the horse, and it was obeying him. He knew how to handle horses! He explained to the man how to control the horse. Dad then told me something I never forgot. He said never trust anyone who was mean to horses or dogs. I know from my life with dogs that what Dad said was 100 percent accurate.

Thinking about Dad and his ability to handle animals from his farm days brings back memories of him and my goat, yes goat! I lived on a very small farm, and my wife wanted a goat. So, we found Hetty, an American Alpine. She was a very large goat and lots of fun. I told Dad about the goat and he wanted to see it.

Dad came to visit, and I took him to see the goat. We all are there, my wife, mother and Dad. He goes over to the goat and looks at it. They are about 10 feet away from each other. Dad leans over and raises his two hands at the goat. He then points at the goat with each pointing finger and makes a strange sound. The goat explodes into action! She reared up on her hind legs, turns sideward, bent her neck and lunged towards Dad. Hetty charged right to him and stopped. The goat was jumping up and down and then started to hop in circles around him. She then backed off and charged him again. This time she lunged right past him. All the time, Hetty was on her two hind legs!

Dad never moved but kept pointing his fingers at the goat while making a strange sound. I yelled thinking the goat was attacking him. Dad laughed and said he was just playing with her! All of us watching were in amazement as the goat stayed on her hind legs and was running around him and even charging him. Dad was laughing real hard and said this is the way he would play with his goats in Ireland! When I think of the way my father communicated with Hetty, it really validated the story about him walking up and touching the wild deer.

For weeks afterwards, I tried to imitate Dad. I would stand with my fingers pointing at Hetty. She paid no attention whatsoever to me, unless I was feeding her! I and my wife still talk about how my dad played with Hetty. In addition to all the amazing abilities of Dad, he was an expert with horses and goats!

Another feat of Dad's, that may even surpass his amazing power, was his ability to eat enormous amounts of food. Dad's ability to consume food was legendary with all who knew him. We would marvel at how much he could eat, especially breakfast. He remained a great eater right up to his passing at age 94!

Dad ate enormous amounts of food but always good food. I never knew him to eat ice cream, cakes, or candies. He drank lots of coffee but always without sugar. I also never remember him drinking soda. Dad would find the best meat market and bakery, and this was where he would buy his food. It was always the best food he could find. He also would find the best restaurants in the area. He knew the best ones for miles around.

Breakfast is what set my father apart from mere mortals. He would start every morning with a large mixing bowl of oatmeal. He loved oatmeal. On the top, he would put wheat germ and cream. This alone was enough for six people! He called the oatmeal "stir about". After finishing the oatmeal, it was on to the eggs. He had a minimum of four eggs but more depending on how hungry he was. Then there was the bacon or sausage. The amount depended on how hungry he was! He called it slabs of bacon. There was the toast to go with the eggs. Again, it was two slices, or more depending on how hungry he was. Dad was often real hungry! He had lots of butter on the toast. There was no telling how many cups of coffee he drank for breakfast! All told, I would estimate he ate enough for breakfast to feed six to eight people. I would just marvel at how much food he could consume for breakfast. Remember, this was every day and he looked so thin. There was never any fat on my father, never.

Around lunch time, he claimed he was starving! He usually did not eat a huge lunch compared to breakfast, but it still was a lot of food. Then came dinner, he loved roast beef and steak, so, that was often for dinner. There were potatoes and turnips, so they were piled high on his plate. He would eat lots of bread with, of course, many cups of coffee. At dinner, he probably only ate as much as three people.

When Dad was younger and into his 50s, his snack before bed really set him apart from mere mortals. At dinner time, he would boil an extra potato. Then just before bed, he would cook a small steak. So his bedtime snack was a steak and boiled potato with lots of butter!

The following two examples highlight Dad's legendary ability to eat. I would take the grandchildren to visit him every summer and take the kids to some place or event. This particular summer we decided to go to the Baseball Hall of Fame in Cooperstown. In the morning, Dad ate his average enormous breakfast.

After breakfast, Mom packed several brown paper shopping bags full of sandwiches and fruit. When sandwiches were made for Dad, they were not a slice or two but thick!

I have no idea how many sandwiches were made, but there were lots. It seems we were gone only a short time, maybe 30 minutes, when he became hungry. I was driving so one of the kids started to feed him. I remember eating one or two sandwiches on the way and probably the kids each had one. Dad ate all the rest! Then he was into the fruit! I watched him eating apples and bananas. When we arrived at Cooperstown, all the food was gone, all of it! He then told me to look for a place for lunch! I told him no, he had enough to eat! I can remember that day like it was yesterday.

No matter how sick Dad was he always ate. Once while I was visiting, Dad became ill and could not breathe. He had pains in his chest, so Mom called the EMTs. They came and took him to the hospital. I followed the ambulance and found him in the emergency room. It turns out he had pneumonia. While he is in the Intensive Care Unit, he hears a cart going down the hall. He tells me to go and see if his dinner is on it. I do not move, and he starts yelling at me to move. To quiet him down, I go out into the hall and sure enough there is a food cart! I asked if they had extra food, and the attendant said he could not give out food without a doctor's permission. I explained this to Dad, and it quieted him down. Here he is in the ICU with pneumonia and hears the food cart in the hall and wants to eat!

When Dad was 92, he went into assisted living. This was a great benefit to him. His eating started to slow down some, but he still required more food than the average person. Dad would receive three breakfasts every day, which included oatmeal, pancakes and eggs! He ate like this right to end!

There may have been a few people, pound for pound, stronger than Dad. It is possible that a person could be found that could eat more than him. But, there was no one who sneezed like my dad, no one! The family and everyone that knew him probably could remember the first time they heard him sneeze or had some story about it. His sneeze was the loudest and most powerful you could ever imagine.

He never sneezed just once, but it ended up as a series of maybe four to six. I just cannot imagine anyone sneezing with more force than Dad.

I am not in any way exaggerating about the incredible noise of his sneeze. Never in my life did I ever hear anyone even come close to sneezing like him. When the sneeze started, he would bend over and then started with a noise like "heeeeeeee". It would then turn into a roar, which cannot be described with words other than an explosion. Mom said when he sneezed in the assisted living center; you could hear it all over the floor. Even at 94, with bad lungs, he could sneeze like this!

My outstanding memory of Dad sneezing was the first time I heard him. I was around 12, and we were walking into a store like Walmart. There was an arcade over the main entrance under which vehicles could drive. This arcade was great for magnifying sounds. We were just about to enter the store when Dad put out his hand and stopped me. He said nothing, but bent down like he was going to pick something up. All of a sudden he shot upwards with this explosion of a sneeze. I looked in horror, as did all the people around us! Dad said nothing but bent over again. Then he shot upwards and roared again. I literally thought he was exploding and ran from him. I went up against the wall and stood frozen watching in horror! Then he did it again and again. By this time, there was a large crowd standing watching him. He called to me, and at first I would not come as I was really afraid. He yelled at me and I came. He said he was weak and had to go back to the car and rest. That was the end of our shopping.

My dad did not even sneeze normally! Could anyone sneeze louder than this? The episodes reported are just the tip of the iceberg. I did not live with my father, but if I had, how many other stories could be added? How many stories could co-workers tell! How about all his friends growing up in Ireland? Dad truly was one-of-a-kind.

Chapter Four

A New Species

As incredible as my father's physical strength and eating abilities were, his medical history was almost beyond belief. It starts when he was in the military during World War II. I never fully understood what happened, but somehow he had a severe stomach operation, which he was not supposed to survive. This operation involved ulcers. He ended up with a medical disability and under the medical care of the Veterans Administration for the rest of his life.

All his life he survived one life threatening issue after another. He had two major cancer operations, one when he was 86, and survived both without chemo! There were three major stomach operations, along with almost not surviving having his gall bladder removed. It was so infected the poison spread throughout his body. Another time, he also nearly died from food poisoning and blood poisoning. This is just a brief overview of his medical history!

When Dad was first operated on for ulcers, he was not expected to live. He was hemorrhaging severely and it could not be stopped. He was in bed with a nurse sitting next to him on a chair. He believed she was there for a "death watch". He wanted her out of the room; because he felt if she left he would live. It took all his strength to call her. She came and he asked her to leave, which she refused. It took the longest time to get enough strength to call her the second time. He finally called and she came over. He again asked her to leave and she said "no". He asked her to come closer. When she did, he spit and told her to leave. She immediately left, and he lived through the night and fully recovered.

As Dad recovered, he was addicted to morphine. He could not live without it. Dad was sent to a special military hospital to break the addiction. It was really difficult to break the hold morphine had over him. All he lived for was the morphine. He would get anxious and be soaked in perspiration waiting for the next shot. He would sit and just look at the clock waiting for the shot.

A doctor took an interest in Dad and personally worked with him to break the addiction. It took about three months to finally gain the victory. For the rest of his life, he was deeply concerned about being addicted to drugs and would not take pain killers because of this fear.

When I was six in 1954, my mother was preparing me for his death. He had a major stomach operation for cancer and, once again, the doctors could not stop the hemorrhaging. He was in the hospital around Christmas. I remember this as if it was yesterday. It was Christmas day and everyone was telling me that Joe was going to die. I was continually asking questions about him and why was he going to die. I was so troubled that the excitement of Christmas meant nothing.

The doorbell rang and my mother answered. She called me to the door and there stood Uncle Tom Kelly: Dad's brother-in-law. He was holding a big red sled. My mother asked him in but he refused. He said he had spoken to my dad, who was very sorry he could not see me. Uncle Tom mentioned nothing about Dad dying.

Early in the year, I had told Dad that I wanted a sled for Christmas. Dad had requested Uncle Tom to get this sled for

Johnny Mac With the Christmas Sled

me. He then handed me the sled and said this was from Joe. The sled was as big as me! I took it and then watched him get into his car and drive off. I then turned to my mother and said, "See he is alive, he is not going to die!" Again, against all odds, my dad survived and lived to be almost 95!

In looking back over Dad's life and all the stomach and digestive related troubles, I think he was suffering from the ravages of the Helicobacter pylori bacteria. It is more commonly known as H. pylori. The vast majority of stomach ulcers are caused by these bacteria along with it being the leading cause of stomach cancer. This was not known when Dad had these operations. I suggest that anyone reading this that has chronic digestive problems, immediately be checked for H. pylori. It can be treated with antibiotics.

Dad's digestive problems continued for a good part of his life. He developed severe pain in the middle of his chest. At first the doctors thought it was the heart. On one occasion, he was walking down the sidewalk and collapsed in pain. He was barely conscious when a police officer arrived and thought he was a drunken "street person" and tried to force Dad off the sidewalk. Finally, the police officer called the EMTs, who took Dad to the hospital. He called and I went to see him. This was about the third time for this severely painful attack. The doctors could find nothing wrong. I stood next to his bed and said it was the gall bladder. Dad claimed the doctors ruled this out.

It turns out that it was the gall bladder, but Dad would suffer for years before finally the gall bladder was removed. Dad had gall bladder test after test and all were negative. He said no more doctors and no more tests. This went on for about 10 years until one day he fell unconscious. Mom called for the EMTs, and he was rushed to the hospital.

The doctors performed an emergency appendectomy, but that was not the source of the problem. They probed and found that his gall bladder was huge and had ruptured! The poison had started to spread throughout his body. He was within an hour of dying, but was saved by the operation. The next day the doctor was visiting him. While being examined, Dad went into shock! All his vital signs were failing. The doctor said: "He was not going to let this man die". In an emergency, he called for a knife and without any preparation opened Dad up! Dad said the pain was beyond comprehension. It turns out that there was still poison from the gall bladder operation, and it had collected and was seeping into his blood. The doctor's action saved Dad.

This was not the end of his gall bladder problems. He had two more operations that involved his liver. The duct from the liver to the gall bladder became infected which then infected his liver. Once again, he was sick and throwing up and in terrible pain. He was told after the second operation that his liver was damaged, and he would not survive another infection. That was the last liver infection.

Twice he had food poisoning. On one occasion he nearly died. He had eaten at a restaurant and came home. He was lying in bed reading the paper when his stomach began to rise. He could actually watch it swell. He felt sick and began to throw up. He fell on the bathroom floor and could not make it to the telephone he was so weak. He just lay on the floor for a long time, when a friend stopped by. Dad happened to leave the door unlocked and the friend walked in. He was rushed to the hospital, and for a week it was touch and go whether he was going to make it.

Dad had a good friend. This friend's wife was legendary as a terrible cook. He would invite Dad for dinner, but he always made up an excuse to avoid it. Knowing how much my dad loved to eat, she must have been a really awful cook. One day he was visiting, and while there she cooked a steak. Dad said he was trapped and had to eat it. The way Dad described the meat was "shoe leather"! He knew there was trouble because the meat was so difficult to cut. Sure enough, a piece lodged in his throat and he was choking! He could not breathe. It was a long way to the hospital as they lived in the country.

Dad did not think he was going to make it. At the hospital, they could not get the steak out and were going to perform an emergency operation. The doctor put an instrument like a rod in Dad's mouth in an attempt to drive the meat into his stomach. With the last try, the meat dislodged. The doctor told Dad, if the food had been a fraction of an inch higher, he would have choked to death before making it to the hospital! Dad said, his friend never again invited him to dinner!

By profession Dad worked on high pressure steam. In the early 1950s, he was at work when a coworker dropped a huge wrench that hit Dad on the lower back. This created years of pain. In the late 1960s, he was working and tried to move a heavy oil drum. His lower back snapped: he fell unconscious and woke paralyzed. He called me, and I went to the hospital. The doctors could not find what was causing the paralysis which made this very serious. Finally, he was transferred to the veterans hospital in the Bronx where he ended up staying for many months.

Since he was in the hospital so long, I took his dog Teeny home to live with my grandmother. At this time, I think we already had three dogs. Dad had spoiled Teeny, and all she ate was the best steak and roast beef, so she refused to eat our dog food! I still remember grandma saying to the dog "bad luck to you" as she refused the food. After a few days, the dog would eat anything we fed her!

**Classic photo of Joe With His Dogs,
Baby and Brummer.**

Dad was in the hospital for the longest time before the doctors performed a very dangerous test where they drained fluid from his spine and inserted a dye. The test showed two cracked discs that were cutting into his spine. The operation was very dangerous with the possibility he would be paralyzed or even die. Dad had the operation, and I visited him the next day. He was in tremendous pain. This pain would last for years. Dad refused to take pain medication because he was afraid of becoming addicted.

The doctor told Dad he must walk no matter how much pain and no matter how short the distance. He must start immediately, or he would be crippled for the rest of his life. He was told to walk, walk and more walking, as often as he could and as far as he could. Dad did exactly as the doctor prescribed.

He walked all around the Veterans Hospital and learned that the old World War I veterans were not being cared for. The food was brought to them, but many were unable to feed themselves and no one fed them. They were literally starving to death. Dad decided to feed them, and this became part of therapy as he walked around feeding the veterans. He was very upset at these soldiers' lack of care. He asked me to visit him often as veterans, who had no visitors, were neglected.

Dad refused to give in to the pain and walked. This led to a lifetime of walking. He walked every day into his late 70s. I watched him move with incredible pain. Sometimes the pain was so severe that tears would flow, streaming out of his eyes that appeared as if it was from a hose. A puddle of tears would collect at his feet. It seemed after the longest time, perhaps three years, the pain let up. Occasionally, his back would lockup, but for the most part the severe pain was over.

He was severely injured twice at work involving falls. The first was when a scaffold collapsed causing him to fall two stories. He hit the ground and was knocked unconscious. There was no one around, and he lay on the ground for about two hours. When he came to, he had an awful headache and a dent on the side of his forehead! He never went to the doctor, and the dent remained for the rest of his life!

The second injury involved working on a ladder. He was on top of the ladder working over his head. He leaned too far back and lost his balance falling toward the ground back first. He twisted in mid-air hitting the ground and breaking his left arm and nose. He trusted the doctors at the Albany Veterans Hospital, so he decided to drive two hours to Albany! I asked him if the ride was difficult. He said paying the tolls was difficult because he could not use his left hand. His eyes were watering and the nose continually bled. He used lots of tissues!

In 1986, I moved to Nashville, TN. Sometime towards the end of that year, Dad had a heart attack. He was found unconscious in a store. Dad recovered very quickly and we spoke. He said the tests revealed that one-third of his heart was dead, but he felt fine and was not showing any effects of the heart damage. His response about the heart damage was "I still have two-thirds left"!

Living in Nashville was too far from where Dad lived for me to make an easy trip. That special relationship with my father was tugging on me. The Harrisburg, PA office opened, and I decided to take the position, as it was only five hours from him. His heart condition seemed serious, so I wanted to be close by. After moving, I soon went to visit him. The heart damage seemed to have no effect on him. His remedy was to get up early every morning and walk several miles. He took his dogs with him and walked the country roads. I think this strengthened his heart. He never had another attack, and his heart was strong until the very end. The heart attack never slowed him down one bit.

Starting in his 80s, he could not hold down food. He would throw up awful colored bile. This went on for several years, and he was in terrible pain. He had test after test trying to determine what the cause was. The tests found nothing. The doctors gave him medicine that seemed to help for a while. Finally, the doctors found that his stomach had moved as a result of the operation in 1954. His intestines were now being cut off, and this was causing all his digestive trouble.

The problem was his age. He was now in his 80s, and they did not want to operate as it was a major operation. His stomach literally had to be taken out of his body and turned and then replaced! The doctors were concerned he would not survive the operation. They kept on delaying it, but Dad kept on getting sicker and weaker. He was suffering terribly. It became apparent he could not live with this condition, so they decided to operate.

The decision to operate came suddenly. I could not be with him the day of the operation, as I had scheduled speaking engagements. I was with him two days before and planned to come back a few days after the operation. He looked terrible and was extremely weak. One reason for the weakness was anemia. The doctors could not find the cause. The operation was a great success, but during the operation, the doctor found colon cancer, which caused the anemia. The cancer was removed, and Dad refused chemotherapy.

When I visited him in the hospital, he was sitting in a chair and looked 20 years younger! He was excited to see "Johnny". He was very happy as "they were feeding him real good," and he could hold it down. How could this be? He was so much better just two days after this major surgery than before! He was happy and said the only problem was when he stood up "my legs are not under me". It took a while to get his full strength back, but it did come back.

In addition to the stomach troubles, Dad's breathing became a serious issue. These two ailments overlapped. He developed a nasty cough with terrible phlegm. It was getting worse and finally the doctors determined the cause. After World War II, he worked in an air pressurized environment building the tunnels under New York City's East River. He had developed what the doctor called "diver's lungs." It was a form of emphysema where his lungs became rubbery. He had smoked for many years and there was lots of scar tissue. It was 50 years since he worked in the tunnels and 30 years since he stopped smoking, but now in old age the damage was showing up. He was diagnosed with Chronic Pulmonary Fibrosis.

With this lung condition, Dad regularly began to develop pneumonia. Without exaggeration, he was rushed to the hospital at least 20 times with pneumonia or his lungs locked, so that he could not breathe. I worked out a system with Mom whereby if his condition was not serious, she would call and say "Don't worry your dad is in the hospital". If she thought it was serious, she would say: "Your dad is in the hospital, and I think you should come".

There were many times, I would leave immediately and come to the hospital. One occasion stands out in my mind. He had a severe bout with pneumonia and to save his life, the doctor drove a huge needle into his lungs through his back. The doctor then withdrew three liters of fluid! However, the doctor went too deep and damaged Dad. Every time he took a breath, it hurt him. He had to stay in the hospital for several weeks because of the damage.

When you looked at Dad's body, he was like a bionic man. His stomach had scars all over the place! He had them going in every direction and angle, plus he had huge long scars along his spine. I have never seen anyone with the amount of scars as Dad had.

If it was possible for a person to will himself well, it was my father. He truly had an indomitable will. He just took whatever punch life threw at him and kept going. It seemed that no sickness or injury could keep him down. With one-third of his heart dead, he lived like nothing happened. He always got back on his feet to fight another round! He never complained about what was happening. But, through it all, he kept eating, especially breakfast!

There are very few people who live to be 95 and even

fewer with all the medical problems that my father had. His mind was crystal clear right to end without even a slight hint of dementia. He could walk and take care of himself to the end of his life. He was not bedridden. It is really difficult to believe there were many people, who lived to be 95 with all the medical issues that Dad lived through. That indomitable will of his kept him going through everything. Eventually, the Pulmonary Fibrosis proved fatal.

My mother, who lived with Dad through so much, had a unique way of explaining him. She often said that no human being could endure what dad did. She would say in amazement: "Your father is a new species"! I fully agree with her.

Joe at 93 With Tiger Lilly

Chapter Five

Jesus is My Savior

For God so loved the world, that he gave his only begotten Son, that whosoever believeth in him should not perish, but have everlasting life. John 3:16

In 1974, I turned to the Lord Jesus as my Savior. Naturally, I wanted to share the Lord with my dad. This did not turn out as I had hoped. He was hard towards God, very hard. He was not this way when I was younger, but something had changed with him. I am not sure what caused this hardness, but it seemed he changed after the back operation in the late 1960s. For many years that followed, he suffered terrible pain, and this seemed to have changed him. I now realize that he drank alcohol heavily as a form of medication, but around 1974 he completely stopped.

No matter what I said to him about the Bible and Lord Jesus he did not want to hear. He never got ugly with me or asked me to stop. He just would argue and then became very mocking. When he started the mocking, I stopped talking to him about the Bible. I felt it was just making him harder. He did tell me that teaching my children about the Bible was nice, but it was clear that he wanted nothing to do with God. It was strange that he would let me pray with him, but again, he did not want to hear anything about the Bible.

Because the Lord Jesus was so central in my life, it was difficult to drop the topic. It also was odd that I traveled all over the country and spoke about the Lord Jesus and even wrote books, but had no interaction with my father. When traveling, I would always call him. He would ask where I was, but never once asked about my ministry or what I was speaking about. This did cause me sorrow. Looking back at this time, there were occasions when I would sneak a verse in. If I shared anything, it was always John 3:16 and nothing else.

I watched him go through many life threatening issues; issue after issue with a heavy heart that he was not going to make it, and that he would go off into eternity without the Lord as his Savior. Each time, he went to the hospital I wondered if this was the last. I also found that I was unable to speak to him about eternal life. It seems the years of rejection had taken a toll. I could offer a prayer, usually for thanksgiving, but that was all I could do. As time went on, I felt it ever more difficult to even bring up the topic of eternal life with him. This added to the heaviness on my spirit.

Starting about three years ago, I noticed he began to soften towards God. During this time, a Catholic priest visited Dad several times when he was very sick. This had a big impact on him, as he was moved by the priest caring for him. The tension was lessening, but I still was unable to talk with him about eternal life. He was regularly developing pneumonia. Many times he was near death but came back. Each time I would thank the Lord, and tell Dad that Jesus was keeping him alive. He never said anything or asked questions. He never once asked for prayer, but he always let me pray with him.

In mid-January 2012, he was rushed to the hospital with pneumonia. His breathing had stopped, but the EMTs had brought him back! He was in the hospital for two days and demanded to leave. The pneumonia was not fully cleared up, but he wanted out. He went back to the assisted living center.

I called and we spoke. He sounded well. A few days later, his breathing once again stopped. This time he had severe pneumonia in both lungs. The lungs were full of fluid, and he could not breathe on his own.

Mom called and said his condition was very serious. We had spoken so many times in the past about Dad's condition, so that I could tell this was critical. I rushed to the hospital with much prayer. When I got to the hospital, the doctor was just finishing a breathing test, and said Dad could not breathe on his own. A respirator was breathing for him. His heart rate spiked to 135, when he tried to breathe on his own. The doctor said his 95 year old heart could not last long with that high rate.

When I looked at him, I knew this time was different. He was unconscious. His eyes were sunken and both his arms were hideously swollen and discolored, while the legs were swollen, but not nearly as bad as the arms. The swelling was a result of his heart being too weak to handle the IV fluids. His skin was ashen grey. I did not think he could live another day. The doctor decided to keep him on the respirator for four more days. If there was no improvement in his breathing, there was little that could be done for him. The end now appeared very near.

There was little I could do, so I prayed for him. I then went to the top of the bed and stood over him. My mind was racing about what to do. God spoke to my heart and had me quote scripture over Dad. The only verse I could think of was John 3:16. I said it over and over. I had no idea if Dad could hear me, but I just quoted the verse. I sensed little faith to think quoting the verses meant anything.

Because Dad was going to be kept on the respirator for four more days, I decided to go home. I contacted all my friends and many were praying for him from around the world. I have a world-wide Internet ministry, and many of the people following the ministry were praying. There was an overwhelming response for prayer. One group prayed for

Dad's salvation and for a sign I would know it. Both the salvation and sign would come in a very dramatic way.

With so much prayer and the fact that the LORD had kept him alive for so long through so many times he could have died, I did have faith. I admit not much, but I did have hope and faith. The time had arrived to pray with Dad about eternal life in Jesus Christ. It was going to be now or never.

Two days later, my mother called and said his condition was rapidly worsening, and the doctor was going to remove the breathing tube. This was two days ahead of time. Immediately, I headed back to the hospital. Many people called on the way and said they were praying! My mother called and said Dad was breathing without the tube, but I had no idea what his condition was.

When I walked into his room, I expected to see him lying semiconscious. Two days before, he was as close to death as possible. But, there he was sitting up looking 20 years younger! I was stunned by his appearance. His beautiful Irish blue eyes were bright and clear and no longer sunken. Dad's eyes were so blue that you could see them a long way off! Even the swelling in his arms was way down.

He looked at me and yelled, yes yelled with a clear voice, "Johnny, Johnny, Johnny, I knew you would come to see me. Johnny I love you"! I was speechless, as he was not the same man I had seen just two days before! When he called me Johnny, something very special happened inside to my emotions. I felt like when I was 10 year old Johnny with Dad at a Yankee game! That was a very special feeling and now, when he called me Johnny, it triggered the same feeling!

Something wonderful had happened. In his hospital room, I was little Johnny Mac again with my dad. The way he called my name, with all the excitement in his voice took me back to my childhood. I think the Holy Spirit was now using his voice that ministered to me with the words "Johnny I love you son."

I walked around to the side of the bed and said to him, "I

told you Jesus loves you"! He said, "Jesus healed me, it's a miracle". I was even more speechless. Dad had never talked like this his entire life. Here I expected to see him barely alive, and he now is giving glory to the Lord Jesus with a loud clear voice! Even after days of having a tube down his throat, his voice was not raspy but normal. Then he said, "Johnny I know that Jesus hears your prayers". I told him it was a miracle and that great numbers of people from all over the world were praying for him.

What happened next is difficult to express in words because it has a spiritual foundation. He was excited and full of enthusiasm when I asked him if Jesus was his Savior. The power with which he responded was spiritual because of the impact it had on me. He said, "Jesus is my Savior. And I love Jesus and Jesus loves me." He said it with the conviction of someone who had experienced the real love of the Savior in His heart. He said he loved Jesus with such a reality in his voice. I marveled at what he was saying, but more it was the way his words were hitting me.

I then asked him if Jesus died for his sins. He responded with, "Jesus died for my sins. He loves me, and I love him". He mentioned several times that Jesus loved him. Every time he responded to a question, he answered about the love Jesus had for him and that he loved Jesus! Finally, I asked him if he would be in heaven with Jesus. He responded, "Yes, yes, Jesus loves me".

He was sitting up and would thrust his hands up and say with a powerful voice "I'm a new man inside". He was not whispering but speaking with power. My dad knew nothing of the Bible, but what he said was a direct reference to it:

2 Corinthians 5:17 Therefore if any man be in Christ, he is a new creature: old things are passed away; behold, all things are become new.

God had worked in his heart and Dad could feel the reality of the Holy Spirit. Dad spoke with power and joy! Then he said, "I feel power inside me. I feel strong". God was working mightily in his life, and he was telling me what was going on. What was happening was directly out of the Bible. The power he sensed was the resurrection power of the Lord Jesus:

Philippians 3:10 That I may know him, and the power of his resurrection, and the fellowship of his sufferings, being made conformable unto his death;

All Dad wanted to talk about is about how much he loved Johnny and Jesus! Even as I write this, I still marvel what God did for my dad. As far as I am concerned, the LORD raised him from the dead in answer to prayer. There is no natural way he could come out of his condition at 95, and then sit up with a powerful voice shouting in joy. This was a miracle.

Dad's doctor told an amazing story about his medical condition. She was as shocked as I was about the way he responded after having the respirator tube removed. She then said that soon after the tube was removed, Dad went into a catatonic state for over an hour. He lay on the bed with his eyes fixed on the ceiling. He was totally unresponsive to stimulus, including pain stimulus, yet all his vital signs remained normal. She had no medical explanation for this other than a stroke. I knew that he did not have a stroke and told her this. She agreed, but said there was no other medical explanation for what happened.

Looking back at this incident, I believe, during this state, Dad had an encounter with God. This would explain the subsequent joy he had and the love he was manifesting for the Lord Jesus. I did not really lead him to Lord Jesus for salvation, as he was already confessing Jesus when I walked into the room! I did speak John 3:16 over him two days before. Maybe he heard the verse and called on the Lord Jesus in his semi-conscious state? This was puzzling, but I believe it was directly related to this incredible revelation of God's love that my father was now basking in! I never asked Dad if he remembered anything that happened in the catatonic state. He never mentioned it.

In all the years serving the Lord and meeting thousands of people, I never met anyone who was manifesting the love of the Lord Jesus like my dad. You had to be in his presence to fully understand what I am writing. I could sense and receive this love. It was flowing into me as I spoke with him.

What usually happens when a person believes on the Lord Jesus, God gives him a measure of His love. This measure can be understood as an acorn. An acorn grows into a huge oak tree over many years. God gives each person an acorn of His love, which grows over a lifetime. Hopefully, at the end of life, a person is full of God's love. This usually is a slow process, just as a tree grows slowly; however, with Dad he received the entire tree! He was given a full oak tree of love all at once. God's love was so powerful in his life that he could not help but share this with me.

The idea of everyone getting a measure of God's grace follows:

Ephesians 4:7 But unto every one of us is given grace according to the measure of the gift of Christ.

Dad was moved from the Intensive Care Unit to a regular room. My mother and I spoke with the hospice doctor. This doctor said that additional treatment was futile as Dad's heart could no longer pump the IV fluid. This was causing the severe buildup of fluid in his arms and legs. Also, he was suffering from chronic pulmonary fibrosis. His lungs were no longer able to take in oxygen. He no longer could breath and his lungs were full of water.

The doctor then opened Dad's medical records and looked

right at me. He said if I was tested for the CO_2 level in my blood it would be around 35. Incredulously, he said, "Your father's is 135 and that is lowest since he was here"! And, this was after Dad received the highest pressure of oxygen that could be given! A CO_2 blood level of 100 or higher is fatal as life cannot be sustained at this level. Yet, Dad was fully conscious and alert with levels way higher than 100!

The doctor felt that Dad should not be alive, or at least, he should be unconscious. He had never seen anyone with a CO_2 level like this, and yet be alive and as alert and clear thinking as Dad. He was just amazed that Dad was even alive! He went on to say that Dad could die at any moment and surely did not have long to live. We explained to Dad that there was no more treatment for his condition. He did not want any additional treatment. He was at peace with this.

The meeting with the hospice doctor really stunned me as Dad's medical condition came into focus. He was 95 years old and failed every breathing test. He could not take in oxygen on this own. His CO_2 level was an unheard of 135 and even higher. His rasping lungs could be heard five feet away without a stethoscope. And yet, he was not breathing rapidly! With all this going against him, when he spoke his voice was clear and powerful! There was absolutely no weakness in his voice.

When he said, "Jesus loves me and I love Jesus," it was with power! He did not labor to speak at all. His physical condition compared to the power and authority with which he spoke did not add up. I knew God had performed a miracle.

After thinking about what happened to Dad, I believe that he had actually, in a real sense, died. It was God's Holy Spirit now keeping him alive. He was alive by a sovereign act of God. After seeing him and listening to the doctor's report, it was clear to me that a miracle had occurred. God gives everyone natural strength to live with usually 80 years being the limit.

Psalm 90:10 The days of our years are three score years and ten (70); **and if by reason of strength** they be fourscore years (80), yet is their strength labour and sorrow; for it is soon cut off, and we fly away.

Dad had no strength left in his body to live, so for a few days, he was directly being kept alive by the Holy Spirit. This explains the power he had to speak, along with the absolutely clarity of mind, while at the same time having a CO_2 level which at a minimum caused unconsciousness but most likely death.

Several people had seen him before the respirator was removed, including my mother and her sister and brother-in-law. There were friends that also visited him. None of them could believe his recovery and praising Jesus like he was! One called me, and we spoke at length about what happened to Dad. She had seen his condition and felt it was a real miracle.

I spent the next two days with Dad in the hospital. He was in very good spirits and really at peace. Mostly he wanted to talk about love. He was so full of love that he had to talk about it. He would look at me and say, "Johnny loves Joe and Joe loves Johnny". The way he looked at me was special. The look of his eyes and the inflection of his voice made what he was saying special. He would look at Mom and say the same thing. All the nurses heard him say that he loved them. At first, I thought that he was just kidding with the nurses because Dad had a tremendous sense of humor. But, then I thought that when he said he loved them, this was the love of God in his heart coming out!

He continued to talk about that Jesus loved him and he loved Jesus. He always coupled the two loves together. He never once mentioned God, but always used the name of Jesus. The time spent with him was wonderful. Just before leaving him for the last time, I put up my fists and said, "I'm not afraid of you!" He put up his fists and laughed. This was the McTernan greeting we had through the years. Most families hugged when they greeted, but Dad and I would get into a boxing stance with "fists up" making noises like we were ready to fight. I guess that was the Irish in us.

As I was leaving him for the last time and with "hands up," I asked if Jesus was his Savior. Dad looked me right in the eyes and stared at me. He then dropped his hands. He could not say Jesus was his Savior in a fighting stance. He said "Jesus is my Savior". I said that is wonderful Dad. I walked to the end of the bed and looked toward him. Again, he said "Jesus is my Savior". I walked to the door and looked over to him. With a POWERFUL voice, Dad said to me, "Jesus is my Savior". I waved good bye and walked down the hall to the elevator. All the way, I could hear "Jesus is my Savior"! The very best thing I could ever hear from him was "Jesus is my Savior" and "Johnny I love you".

This was the last thing I heard my dad say, "Jesus is my Savior". Two days later, he went into the loving arms of the Blessed Redeemer. I had told the doctors, that when Dad did not eat, it was a sure sign the end was near. The morning of his passing, for the first time ever, he refused breakfast. He then fell asleep and never really woke. Later that evening, with Mom holding his hand, he peacefully passed directly to be with the Lord Jesus, whom he really loved. Dad passed in his own terms. He was free of any medical assistance.

My last memory is standing next to him with the "McTernan hands up" greeting and him saying that Jesus was his Savior. This is the way I will remember him. In a few days, God sure did pack an abundance of spiritual quality into my father's life. I am very thankful to my Father in heaven for what blessings he bestowed on my father. I will greatly miss my dad, but I am not going to look back. I will look forward to the Blessed Hope, which is Jesus coming for those that love Him, and the Marriage Supper of the Lamb in heaven. This is when I will be reunited with him.

At the viewing, everyone shared "Joe McTernan stories", and I learned new ones from his good friend! The new stories fit the pattern of Dad's amazing life. At the funeral, I gave the eulogy. Almost everyone attending knew, at least part of, my dad's incredible life. I zeroed in on the last few days, when he had such an experience with Jesus. I did not preach at all, but just told the story of what happened and Dad's testimony of loving Jesus. I said, without a doubt, that Dad was in heaven because of his testimony that the Lord Jesus was his Savior and for no other reason. It was truly wonderful to give his testimony.

Mom told me that the hospice chaplain had visited Dad and wanted to talk with me. I did call him and had a wonderful conversation. The chaplain said that he spoke with Dad about his salvation and was sure that my father knew the Lord as his Savior. He prayed for Dad who asked him to come back again for additional prayer. It was yet another sign that Dad's heart was right with God, and that he was ready for eternity.

Towards the end of Dad's life, I had a heavy burden for his eternal destiny. In fact, I would say it was a dread. But with the miracle that God performed and Dad's awesome manifestation of Jesus' love, the sting of death was removed from me. The heavy burden is now all gone being replaced with peace. Dad's love ministered to me for those few days. It is also very clear how much more I needed to grow in God's love to reach what Dad had in only a few days!

While he was alive, I would have loved to have worked together with him in my ministry, but this did not happen; however, in a real sense, I now have a ministry with Dad. Although he is in heaven with Jesus, by sharing his testimony, we do have a ministry together. If he did not have a testimony of Jesus' love, we could not have a ministry together: it is his testimony and me sharing it, to the glory of the Lord Jesus that brings us together!

There is a parable in the Bible that applies directly to Dad and what happened to him during his last four days. I had never really given this parable much thought and never had any examples to apply to it. The parable is found in Mathew 20. It is about a man who hires laborers to work for him. He hires some early in the morning, and then, as the day goes, on he hires more until finally near the end of the day he hires more.

When it comes time to pay the workers, he pays them all the same. The ones that worked all day were upset at the ones who were hired at the end and were paid the same full salary. This parable follows:

> Matthew 20:8-9 So when even was come, the lord of the vineyard saith unto his steward, Call the labourers, and give them their hire, beginning from the last unto the first. And when they came that were hired about the eleventh hour, they received every man a penny.
>
> (10) But when the first came, they supposed that they should have received more; and they likewise received every man a penny. (11) And when they had received it, they murmured against the goodman of the house, (12) Saying, These last have wrought but one hour, and thou hast made them equal unto us, which have borne the burden and heat of the day.

The parable goes on that the owner had made a fair contract with each person. In his mercy and grace, he decided to give the last person hired the same amount as all the others. He wanted to bless those that had no work but were hired late in the day. It was the owner's business, and he could pay as he wanted to.

> Matthew 20:13 But he answered one of them, and said, Friend, I do thee no wrong: didst not thou agree with me for a penny? (14) Take that thine is, and go

thy way: I will give unto this last, even as unto thee. (15) Is it not lawful for me to do what I will with mine own? Is thine eye evil, because I am good?

By what happened to my father, I now clearly understand this parable. At the very, very end of the day, God "hired" my dad and paid him an abundant "wage". Although Dad was with the Lord only for a few days, God poured a lifetime of blessings into him! God is sovereign and can do as He pleases. My dad is the perfect example of this parable.

Dad lived to be almost 95. His total life covered 34,698 days. God did this miracle of pouring His love and grace into Dad during a four day span until he died. In terms of Dad's life, this was a miniscule 0.0001152 percent! In this incredibly short time, it almost cannot be measured, God poured out His love into Dad to the point that I have not reached yet. With great power, Dad was saying, "I am a new man inside" and "I feel power inside me"!

Joe and Johnny

The special bond with my Dad that was forged deep in me that fateful day, when I was six, lasted a lifetime. It never broke. To the very end we were Joe and Johnny Mac. We were McTernans.

Chapter Six

God is Love

And we have known and believed the love that God
hath to us. *God is love*; and he that dwelleth in love
dwelleth in God, and God in him.

1 John 4:16

In my dad's presence, you could actually feel the love
pouring out of him. As I mentioned, I am at loss to ade-
quately describe the reality of love that was flowing from
him. I knew that he had a deeper love of God than I possessed. This tangible love was the real love of God. It was
very wonderful to be in the presence of such love. I believe
that Dad had the complete fullness of God's love that a human
could possess.

The above verse mentions that God is love, and a person
that dwells in love dwells in God. This is what I was feeling
from Dad: the real presence of God through love! It was the
love that God has for us as mentioned in this verse. My dad
had a full measure of this love. It was overflowing in him.
God wants to give everyone the fullness of this love. It may
not be as dramatic as what happened to my dad, but God's
love is available to all that seek Him. There are no exceptions.

The reason that people do not experience the fullness of

God's love is a problem called sin. God's love and man's sin do not mix. God's love cannot flow through a heart that is full of selfishness, rebellion, hatred and a host of other issues. God calls this a "stony heart". It is like a hardened stone of granite and stones cannot possess love.

> Ezekiel 36:26 A new heart also will I give you, and a new spirit will I put within you: and I will take away the stony heart out of your flesh, and I will give you an heart of flesh.

Through faith in the Lord Jesus Christ, God takes out the rock hard heart of stone and replaces it with a heart of flesh. It is this heart which can receive God's love. Because Dad had a new heart of flesh, God's love was freely flowing through him. He had a new spiritual heart, and this is why Dad was saying many times, "I am a new man inside"! The heart of flesh is not a theory, but it is a living reality of what happens when a person trusts Jesus Christ as his Savior. Dad became a "new person" through faith in Jesus Christ.

> 2 Corinthians 5:17 Therefore if any man be in Christ, he is a new creature: old things are passed away; behold, all things are become new.

The foundation for obtaining a new spiritual heart and God's love is the confession of Jesus Christ as your Savior. This is exactly what my father did. I asked him if Jesus Christ was his Savior and he said, "Yes". He then publicly made that confession. He was not ashamed of the Lord Jesus.

> Romans 10:9 That if thou shalt confess with thy mouth the Lord Jesus, and shalt believe in thine heart that God hath raised him from the dead, thou shalt be saved.

The confession of Jesus Christ also includes believing that He died on the cross for your sin. Dad had assurance that he was going to be in heaven with Jesus. He knew this because of the realization that he was a sinner and Jesus died on the cross for his sin. The death of Jesus paid the penalty for our sin, which is eternal separation from the God of love. No one can go to heaven without first believing that Jesus died for his sin.

Once the penalty is paid for, God is now free to pour His love into us. This was exactly what happened to my dad. I asked Dad if Jesus died for his sin, and immediately he answered "Yes", and added with great excitement "Jesus loves me".

2 Corinthians 5:21 For he hath made him to be sin for us, who knew no sin; that we might be made the righteousness of God in him.

The last question I asked Dad was if he had assurance of being in heaven with Jesus. Without hesitation Dad said emphatically "Yes," and then followed with "Jesus loves me and I love Jesus". There was absolutely no doubt in Dad's mind that he had eternal life because Jesus was his Savior, and now there was a powerful love bond between them. Dad was dwelling in the fullness of God's love, so there was no doubt in his mind. Dad did not know Bible doctrine that gave him this assurance. It was the power of God's love in his heart that gave him this assurance. He was dwelling in God's love which was enough assurance for him!

Romans 10:13 For whosoever shall call upon the name of the Lord shall be saved.

Dad is a great example of God's mercy that, even at the very last moments of his long life, he was able to trust in

Jesus Christ as his Savior. I did not get a chance to ask Dad the question, if he wished he would have trusted in Jesus way earlier in life. But, I am sure that he wished he would have. No matter what stage of your life you are now in, it is never too late or too soon to trust in Jesus Christ as your Savior. But, why would anyone delay and miss the love of Jesus in their heart and as well, the assurance of eternal life? These both are free gifts from a loving Father God.

Dad received a full measure of God's love all at once. God gives a measure of His love exactly as each person needs it. Usually the measure is as an acorn that continually grows over a lifetime. If you trust Jesus Christ as your Savior, God will give you that measure of love. As you grow in Jesus you will grow in His love.

I witnessed the full love of God in my dad. I wish that everyone could obtain such love and have assurance of eternal life with Jesus. There is only one way to obtain this, and that is through the confession that Jesus Christ is your Lord and Savior. The bottom line is to trust in the Lord Jesus and only Him because He is the true source of love and eternal life.

John 3:16 For God so loved the world, that he gave his only begotten Son, that whosoever believeth in him should not perish, but have everlasting life.

Chapter Seven

Jesus Came to Heal the Brokenhearted

"He hath sent me to heal the brokenhearted"
Luke 4:18 (KJV)

The Divorce

For the LORD, the God of Israel,
saith that he hateth putting away Malachi 2:16

My parents' divorce had a huge impact on me. The blame - game about who caused the divorce is irrelevant, but it left me very confused and living with my mother against my will. It was not that my mother was mean to me; rather, I felt that I did not fit or belong in her new family. The incident with my stepfather had a huge impact on my life that changed it forever. I am sure that he did this for unity in the family and not to hurt me, but this was a traumatizing byproduct of the divorce. My will was sealed, as I wanted to be with my dad but could not, and nothing could take the place of being with him. I grew up as a "fish out of water".

Most people have no idea how deep the chaos and trauma a divorce can bring into a child's life, unless they have lived through it. It can cause great pain and trauma to a child. The effects of a divorce can cause lifetime damage that only God's Holy Spirit can heal. It affects the spiritual heart, which no amount of psychiatry or drugs, whether legal or illegal, can heal. The divorce causes spiritual problems, and this is at the root of the damage.

The Bible speaks directly to the issue of a divorce. God has very strong words about divorce and warns about the dangers of what it causes. The Bible actually states in Malachi 2:16 that God hates divorce, and it leads to violence. The violence can be covered over outwardly, but internally, in one's spirit, there is violence. This is exactly what happened to me. I could sense my mother's hatred for my father, and it greatly impacted me as a young child.

Malachi also states that when husband and wife are one, they produce a godly seed or child. In this atmosphere, a child can then grow up to be godly; however, divorce severely interferes with this process, as it creates an atmosphere of violence. This atmosphere wreaks havoc on a developing child. This is exactly what happened to me. I could sense my mother's hatred for my father along with my stepfather's attitude, both impacted me greatly as a young child. It added to a broken heart.

Three times in this section of scripture the Bible makes the connection between the human spirit and divorce. In this section of the Bible divorce is referred to as "putting away". These verses from Malachi follow:

Malachi 2:14 Yet ye say, Wherefore? Because the LORD hath been witness between thee and the wife of thy youth, against whom thou hast dealt treacherously: yet is she thy companion, and the wife of thy covenant. (15) And did not he make one? Yet had he the residue of the **spirit**. And wherefore one? That he might seek a godly seed. Therefore take heed to your **spirit**, and let none deal treacherously against the wife of his youth.

(16) For the LORD, the God of Israel, saith that he hateth putting away: (divorce) for one covereth violence with his garment, saith the LORD of hosts: therefore take heed to your **spirit**, that ye deal not treacherously.

The problems caused by a divorce are both physical and spiritual. Most of the problems can only be fully cured spiritually. Since God hates divorce, He will work greatly in the hearts of a husband and wife with a troubled marriage, if they let Him. In today's society, divorce is so common that it is not looked upon by many as being a serious problem. But, to God it is very serious as a marriage where the husband and wife work as one is the very foundation of society. If the marriage unit breaks down, a society will crumble. This is at the very heart of most of America's problems. Americans are paying a huge price because of the breakdown of the family unit and its effect on the children. If possible, avoid a divorce at all cost.

There are six issues that a divorce can destroy in the lives of those involved. If anyone reading this is contemplating a divorce, please consider these issues:

Spiritual: The divorce will affect your relationship with God as He hates divorce.

Physical: The stress of going through a divorce can be devastating on the body. It is especially hard for a man. The median age of death for a divorced man is 57.

Emotional: Divorce can lead to serious emotional problems including depression and alcohol or drug abuse.

Legal: There can be all sorts of legal issues with a divorce.

Financial: It can create a quick way into poverty or a serious reduction in a standard of living.

Children: A divorce can devastate children, as I am a living example. It is very easy for a child from a divorce to become brokenhearted, and this is exactly what happened to me.

If you have been damaged by a divorce, it is time to come to God through Jesus Christ and ask Him to heal you. Remember, divorce can cause spiritual problems in the heart, which can only be healed by God working in a person's life.

The Brokenhearted

Keep thy heart with all diligence;
for out of it are the issues of life. Proverbs 4:23

Because of the divorce, I grew up with a broken heart that continued into a good part of my adult life. The strange thing about living with a broken heart from childhood is that I did not know that I had one! It was just a normal life, as I never experienced life without a broken heart. I learned to adapt to the broken heart and would cover it over.

Throughout my life there was something wrong inside only I did not know what it was. I could not pinpoint the source, but there was something unsettled in my soul. The best way to describe the problem was like driving your vehicle with the emergency brake on. The car is moving and has lots of power, and yet something is holding it back. This was the way I felt about life and had absolutely no idea what was causing it.

One day I was listening to a radio interview of the author Elizabeth Marquardt. She was being interviewed about her book *Between Two Worlds: The Inner Lives of Children of Divorce*, 2005, Crown Publishers. (I highly recommend this book). As Marquardt spoke, I was riveted, because she was describing what was going on inside me. She had touched that feeling that I was living life with "the emergency brake on". She explained this was very common in children from a divorced family to feel there was something wrong and yet not know what it was. Then she zeroed on the root of the problem: that divorce can cause a child to become broken-hearted, and this wounded heart can be carried into adulthood. From both Marquardt's interview and book, I finally had a clear picture of what happened to me. The divorce created a broken heart, and this was the source of living with "the emergency brake on!" I knew Luke 4:18 and that the Lord Jesus came to heal the brokenhearted. Immediately I prayed and asked the Lord to heal my broken heart. What happened next was strange. I began to feel extremely lonely. In fact, the loneliness at one point became overwhelming. Marquardt did mention that a feeling of loneliness was very common in children from a divorce.

This feeling seemed to be at the root of the problem. Loneliness was lodged in my heart, and I had no idea. This loneliness was spiritual and not just the emotion of missing someone. This was the type of loneliness that often accompanies the loss of a spouse. The loss creates a broken heart, and that is why a surviving spouse often soon passes away. This is a deep, deep spiritual loneliness.

As I examined myself, I realized that I could feel lonely in a crowd of people. The feeling of loneliness was always with me! What is so amazing is that until this was revealed to me, I could not see it in my life. It seemed the more I prayed the more lonely I began to feel. It took several weeks of prayer but finally this intense loneliness broke. I could actually feel it leave me, and the healing of my heart began.

God was in the process of knitting together my broken and shattered heart. The feeling of living my life with "the emergency brake on" was gone and I was free. This healing of my heart could only be accomplished spiritually by the power of Jesus Christ. Remember, the root of the problem was spiritual and all other attempts for healing only mask the problem.

There is very little if any preaching and teaching about the

Lord Jesus healing the brokenhearted. There are many ways taught that might manage the bondage, suffering and pain of a broken heart. These usually are found in three or five steps to making a person feel better. These programs can never get at the root of what is troubling a person, if the cause is a broken heart.

There is something very important about healing the brokenhearted and the Bible. Unfortunately, the modern translations, including the very popular New International Version (NIV), omits from Luke 4:18, "he hath sent me to heal the brokenhearted". For this reason and many others, I do not recommend these modern translations but highly suggest that you use the King James Bible. I know the impact of "he hath sent me to heal the brokenhearted" on my life, and it angers me that the modern versions removed this. This omission can result in many people living in the bondage of being brokenhearted.

With the prevalence of divorce today, the amount of children and adults with a broken heart must be staggering. I have focused on divorce but there are numerous other ways a person can develop a broken heart. Without spiritual protection, life is almost designed to break one's heart. It could be broken by a parent, spouse, child, divorce, close friend, death of a loved one, abortion, financial disaster, military combat and a host of other ways.

The good news is that no matter how one's heart was broken, the Lord Jesus came to heal the brokenhearted! There are no exceptions to this. Everyone whose heart was broken can be healed. The center of His ministry was to heal those whose inner being was torn or crushed with a broken heart. This shows God's love for mankind as He does not want us to live brokenhearted.

The Bible, in both the Old and New Testaments, states that Jesus Christ came to heal the brokenhearted:

Isaiah 61:1 The Spirit of the Lord GOD is upon me; because the LORD hath anointed me to preach good tidings unto the meek; *he hath sent me to bind up the brokenhearted,* to proclaim liberty to the captives, and the opening of the prison to them that are bound.

Luke 4:18 The Spirit of the Lord is upon me, because he hath anointed me to preach the gospel to the poor; *he hath sent me to heal the brokenhearted,* to preach deliverance to the captives, and recovering of sight to the blind, to set at liberty them that are bruised,

In the entire Bible, the word brokenhearted is found only in these two verses. The Old Testament it is prophetic foretelling Jesus Christ's coming. Both times it refers to His ministry. There is no doubt that God sent Him to heal the brokenhearted.

When both the Hebrew and Greek words translated "brokenhearted" are examined, a very clear picture is given to show exactly what is a broken heart. The Hebrew reveals a very violent act of breaking. It is associated with "to rend violently, crush and shatter". The Greek gives the same view of the inner heart being broken into pieces with slivers.

A broken heart is very serious. It is not just slightly hurt or merely bruised but has been violently crushed and shattered. Looking at it physically, it is as if the bones of a leg were crushed and shattered into splinters through a violent accident. This is what the Lord Jesus came to heal: a heart that has been torn apart into splinters.

Isaiah 61:1 says that Jesus came to bind the brokenhearted, while Luke 4:18 uses the word heal. This word means literally to heal and make whole, which is exactly what a broken heart needs. It needs to be healed in the same way that a broken leg needs healing. Brokenhearted people need a spiritual healing, which is very similar to a physical healing for broken bones. In fact, a shattered and splintered broken leg is a great example of what a broken heart spiritually resembles.

Isaiah 61 uses bind rather than heal. To bind gives the image of being wrapped tightly or being compressed as in a cast. This is exactly what a broken and splintered heart needs to heal. All the splinters need to be set back in place and then tightly bound, so it can correctly heal. This is how God spiritually heals a broken heart.

A broken heart causes severe emotional pain just as a broken and splintered leg brings intense physical pain. Think of a shattered leg that never healed and all the pain this creates. If a person constantly walked on the leg and never gave it time to heal, this person would suffer greatly. He could learn to adapt, so he might limp around and move like a "car with the emergency brake on". He could be powerful with the potential to be a great runner, yet the shattered leg holds him back. This is precisely the way a person is with a broken heart.

Once the heart is bound and healed, the emotional pain leaves. The issues that caused the broken heart no longer have a hold, and a person is now free to live in the peace of God. Many people can actually feel when God heals their heart and frees them, just as a person would know when the pain stopped from a broken bone. It is so comforting to know that God loves us so much that He sent the Lord Jesus to heal the brokenhearted.

Examples of God Healing the Brokenhearted

When God healed me of a broken heart, He also called me into a ministry of helping those that are brokenhearted. I have great faith that when I pray for someone with a broken heart; that God will move to heal it. When I speak I often end with a call to heal anyone who is brokenhearted. Sometimes when ministering to a person the word brokenhearted flashes across my mind. There may be no external sign that this person is brokenhearted, but I will mention it. Each time, the person admitted that his/her heart was broken.

What I found, without exception, is that, when people realize they have a broken heart, with great detail, they can recall when it happened and what caused it. This even could mean going way back into childhood. It is amazing to listen to the great detail of what caused a broken heart.

The event traumatized the person, and it is burned into the memory along with the emotions that accompany it. When God heals the broken heart, He also heals the emotions. This is what frees the person of the pain. In my case, I could remember back to when I was six and the event with my stepfather as the very root of the broken heart. The following are three examples of my ministering to people with a broken heart.

The first was when I was speaking at a Bible conference, and a pastor that I knew attended it. We were sitting in a restaurant when a young woman sat with us. She was a friend of the pastor. He told me that he had ministered to her for a while without success. She loved the Lord Jesus but had no inner peace. I remember that she was well dressed and attractive with no outward sign of inner distress.

As I was listening to the pastor and young woman speak, the word brokenhearted flashed into my mind. I opened my Bible to Luke 4:18 and told her that I think she was suffering from a broken heart. She then stared right at me and said without hesitation said "Yes I am". She intensely focused on every word I spoke to her.

She immediately knew she had a broken heart and what caused it. She did not want to go into details of being brokenhearted, but she knew the event that caused it. I had her read Luke 4:18 and then asked her if Jesus Christ came to heal her broken heart? She said "Yes," and we then prayed. As we prayed she began to say, "I am free, I am free". A great look of joy came over her, and she stood up and said "I am now free, thank you," and she walked away. She knew she was free as the Lord Jesus had just healed her broken heart. She knew it! It was that simple.

The second person was Paul. He was the very good friend of a pastor friend of mine. I had met Paul a few times but did not know much about him. We were at a prayer meeting and Paul was sitting next to me. As we were praying, I could hear Paul pray and knew that something was wrong. After the prayer meeting, I mentioned to Paul what I heard him say. Pastor Jeff told me there was a problem with Paul, and they had been praying 25 years for the victory. They had given up and figured that when Paul was with Jesus, he would know what caused this problem.

I said we needed to pray, and as I started to pray broken-hearted flashed into my mind. I stopped and said to Paul, "You have a broken heart". Instantly and without hesitation, he said, "Yes I do," and he knew exactly when it occurred. He was 12, and it had to do with severe rejection by his mother. Paul was now 65 and yet could remember vivid details of this incident! Pastor Jeff was astonished, as he has no idea that Paul was brokenhearted. I prayed with Paul, and instantly you could see his countenance change! He was set free.

I followed Paul's progress through Pastor Jeff. Paul's mind had been confused, but when his spiritual heart was healed his mind became crystal clear. Pastor Jeff was just amazed at this. Paul truly was set free and even went back to his mother with whom he had no relationship. He had forgiven her. Now with a healed heart Paul could deal with his mother, and their relationship was healed! Paul became close to his mother after being estranged from her for so many years. The catalyst for this was the healing of Paul's broken heart. Paul now lives in God's peace, which had been so elusive for him those many years.

The third is Joni. On my blog, John McTernan's Insights,

there is a Comment Section. I monitor this section to make sure that only proper comments were posted. I began to notice that Joni was posting comments about anxiety attacks. These comments caught my attention, so I contacted her. She told an incredible testimony of things that happened in her life that triggered these anxiety attacks and the medication she was taking. I offered to minister to her about these attacks and she agreed.

It appeared that Joni was suffering from fear, so I prepared scriptures that addressed fear. I had them all ready for the next day. Early in the morning when it was still dark, God woke me with just one scripture for Joni. God impressed on me that she had a broken heart, and clearly I was to give her Luke 4:18 with "he hath sent me to heal the brokenhearted".

The next day I spoke with her about what had happened and shared Luke 4:18. I told her that she was brokenhearted and that this was the root of the trouble and not anxiety. She immediately agreed and knew what caused the broken heart and when it happened.

Her father's first family, with a wife and three children, were all killed in a fire. This left a pall which carried over to the new family. This created great sorrow that affected her heart. It broke her heart that her brothers and sisters were all killed.

When she was about six years old, her father was arrested in her sight. The police grabbed him and were so rough that they ripped the buttons off his coat. He went to jail and her mother would take Joni to visit him in prison. The incarceration and visitations broke her heart. It was this incident that really was the foundation for her living brokenhearted. This broken heart would last her entire life until Jesus healed it.

Years later, her dad was pardoned by the governor and the sheriff, who had her father arrested, went to jail for corruption. Even though her dad was pardoned the damage was done to her spiritual heart.

There were events all though her life that continually rein-forced the broken heart, but one event really crushed it and started all the anxiety attacks. Her sister was brutally mur-dered and this incident simply crushed her heart. She was paralyzed inside and it triggered the severe anxiety attacks. She was taking powerful drugs to try and control this anxiety and had become almost housebound because of the fear. The drugs were of very little help. She had lived like this for seven years.

After listening to this testimony, we prayed, and I asked the Lord to heal her broken heart. A few days later she could sense that something strange was happening in her chest. There was a weird feeling that was starting to scare her. She went to bed and covered herself up with blankets because she was feeling very cold to the point of shaking. She knew this was not an anxiety attack but thought it might be a physical heart attack. She then grabbed her King James Bible and held it close to her chest.

Joni then thought of me and what was happening to her was a result of praying to heal her broken heart. She wanted me to stop praying because the sensation was so powerful. I told her it was God burning the spirit of fear out of her. She went back to bed and now a warm feeling flowed through her chest where her spiritual heart was located. She asked God to stop and the sensation then ended.

Joni realized that God indeed had touched her heart as the terrible anxiety attacks had stopped. She could not drive a car on her own without taking anxiety medicine. Now she was free as the anxiety had left her. Once God healed her heart, the fear and anxiety left. She was now free.

Looking back at my own father's life, there was no doubt that he was living with a broken heart. I never spoke with my dad about having a broken heart, I know that the divorce broke it and maybe other events before and after were part of it. Dad is the perfect example of God's grace, mercy and love for us. God's grace was extended to the very last few days of his life. God's mercy was shown by how completely He healed Dad's shattered heart. God's love was shown by how He so overwhelmingly filled Dad with His peace and joy.

My father's heart was so completely healed that he was saying with great joy, "I am a new man inside". In my mind's eye I can still see Dad lying in bed raising his hands and with a strong voice saying, "I am a new man inside," and "I feel power inside me". God did a complete spiritual healing of my father's heart. If God did this for my dad, He can do it for anyone.

In four short days, God's plan of salvation was manifested in my father. With his confession of Jesus Christ as his Lord and Savior, Dad received the assurance of eternal life with God. He fully understood that Jesus Christ died on the cross for his sins. At the same time, God healed his spiritual inner heart and created a new heart in him that was full of power. This is the real gospel of Jesus Christ: assurance of eternal life and God's power in your life, now!

I am sure that my father would have regretted that he did not confess Jesus Christ as his Savior much earlier in his life. He could have lived in God's love, peace and joy. Please do not delay as my father did, but trust Jesus Christ now. Do you have a broken heart? Now is the time to give this shattered heart to God and have it bound and healed by Jesus Christ. This is what He came to do: heal the brokenhearted. My father is the very best example, which can possibly be given, to prove that this is exactly what Jesus Christ will do to all who come to Him.

"The Spirit of the Lord *is* upon me ...
he hath sent me to heal the brokenhearted"

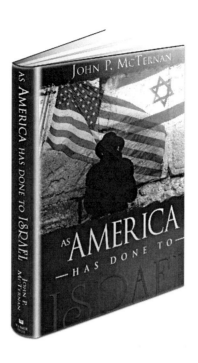

The Book That Proves
the Hand of God on America

There is a direct correlation between the alarming number of massive disasters striking America and her leaders pressuring Israel to surrender her land for peace. Costing hundreds of lives and causing hundreds of $billions worth of damage, dozens of disasters, including devastating earthquakes, raging fires, hurricanes, floods, tsunamis, and tornadoes, have hit America - and always within twenty four hours of putting pressure on Israel. What can you do as an individual - and what can America do - to change the direction of our country in relation to Israel to prevent an increasing number of calamities?

Go to: *USAProphecy.com* to order the book, or my blog: *JohnMcTernan.name*

CPSIA information can be obtained at www.ICGtesting.com
Printed in the USA
BVOW080433090413

317632BV00001B/1/P

9 781622 304257